ESCAPE FROM FACEBOOK

"The Back Home Strategy"

Deliverance from Facebook, fake clicks, bots and other lies.
A survival guide for those who thought that
a social network is all it takes to do digital marketing.

Marco Camisani Calzolari

Published by

MCC Worldwide Digital Consulting

CONTENTS

Chapter 2
The Moment of Truth

2.1. The Show is Sold Out but the Audience is Bored

2.1.1. Facebook is not free!
2.1.2. I don't want to be friends with my butter!
2.1.3. Fans: fanatic or apathetic?

2.2. Does Advertising on Facebook Really Work?

2.2.1. My kingdom for a click
2.2.2. An army of robots clicking on your ads

2.3. The Myth of Social Commerce

2.4 ROI: Return of Illusions

2.5. Bots, Fake Comments, and Paid Reviews

2.5.1. You too are charmed by big numbers
2.5.2. Bots
2.5.3. On a hunt for fakes

2.6. Prisoners of Facebook

2.7. The Death of Facebook

Chapter 3
Adapt or Die: a new strategy

3.1. The Back Home Strategy

3.1.1. Ye were not made to live like unto brutes

3.1.2. Digital survival strategies

3.1.3. What is the Back Home Strategy?

3.1.4. Back Home Strategy tools

3.1.5. Choose your users

3.1.6. Why people should come to me

3.1.7. Who's who of the Back Home Strategy

3.1.8. Is the Back Home Strategy for me?

Introduction

As a professional, popularizer and above all an enthusiast of digital culture, I am quite disconcerted lately by the way companies have been blindly leaping onto the bandwagon of social media marketing with little or no apparent forethought. The most recent trend is to set up a page on Facebook or Twitter and then go about trying to drum up fans and followers, often with no clear strategy beyond that.

And so I have set out to produce a complete (but by no means super-galactic) guide for companies on the informed use of social media. My aim here is to help them recalibrate their expectations and objectives in the face of so much hype.

But don't get me wrong: I firmly believe in social media and their potentials in digital marketing. They are extraordinary tools for achieving grand objectives. They make it possible to engage customers in dialog and get their feedback, with important mutual benefits. They are excellent for Customer Relations Management, generating brand awareness, and promoting products or services. They are also a formidable tool for "pure" marketing. The whole trick is to grasp their real potentials, especially those relating to Facebook.

To do so, it is necessary to open one's eyes and look beyond the easy objectives and the "social media packages" hawked by digital agencies (not all of them paradigms of professionalism). It is necessary to regain control of social media, to use them instead of being used by them. Because what I often see happening is that companies become slaves to these platforms, to their logic, metrics, and interests.

Often poorly advised, companies risk wasting the opportunity to use social networks to their advantage. They make Facebook into their one and only (or main) digital front office, with the sole apparent objective of pumping up the numbers of their sterile, useless, and totally bored fans.

I love Facebook. I use it all the time and to great advantage. I am really sorry that others can't seem to do the same. That's why I want to talk about a new approach to this digital wonderland: the Back Home Strategy.

Within this strategy, social networks, and Facebook in particular, become part of a complex strategy that integrates audience feedback and increasing brand awareness with the creation of a very specific and detailed database in order to maximize the effectiveness of more traditional and effective forms of direct marketing, such as Direct Email Marketing (DEM).

For this to happen, the company must set up a central Home and then bring users (back) there through its many channels, which are all solidly connected to social networks but completely distinct from them. This Home has to represent the company on the web in an official and un-ambiguous way, encompassing and uniting the company website, associated blogs and forums, extensions of the website dedicated to special projects, e-commerce store, as well as branded communities and branded social networks. In short, it has to be a place that exists and can be inhab-ited regardless of whether there is a Facebook out there or not.

In the first part of the book we will talk about the siren song of social media marketing: why have social networks become so trendy that they are now seen as an absolute must? Why are almost miraculous virtues ascribed to them? How did social media marketing gain its awesome and legendary status? Are there really such things as influ-encers?

We will pick out specific flaws in the second chapter, de-bunking the most common illusions and highlighting the most frequent errors. There will also be an analysis of the mirages, pitfalls, and unfounded claims abounding on social networks, including the well known question of fake fans and fake followers. We will also ponder the future of social networks: what would happen if Facebook suddenly disappeared?

Lastly, in Chapter 3, I will make some concrete proposals as to what can be done to reap the potentials of social media: implementation of the Back Home Strategy.

It is my hope that this book will represent useful and valuable help on the road to enlightenment so that companies can deftly negotiate what might appear to be an impenetrable jungle. By the end of the book, I hope I will have made it clear to marketing managers that Facebook is a means and not an end.

But a few words of thanks are in order before we get on with it. I want to thank my life companion, who doesn't like to be out in the spotlight but has stood behind every one of my small or large successes. She is my source of inspiration and she keeps me on an even keel. I am what I am thanks to her. And this book is what it is thanks to Alice Mascheroni, who has provided inestimable support in researching and writing it.

ESCAPE FROM FACEBOOK

Convictions are more dangerous enemies of truth than lies.
Nietzsche

Chapter 1
The Siren Song

1.1. Social Networks, yes or no

1.1.1. The great exodus to social networks

What is a social network?

Social networks are not yet another innovation of the digital age, they have deep roots in sociology. As I explained in the book *Impresa 4.0*[1], a social network is any group of people who are interconnected by various bonds, ranging from casual acquaintance to families ties. The concept is often used as a structural element in intercultural studies carried out by sociologists and anthropologists.

The online version of social networks is one of the most evolved forms of communication online. Indeed it has evolved past the bounds of the "150 rule" (Dunbar number), violating the principle by which the maximum number of people with whom an individual can maintain stable social relationships is in the neighbourhood of 150.

Online social networks have a long history (by modern terms) dating back to the late 1980s with the IRC (Internet Relay Chat) protocol, which allowed users to chat as well as share files and links. In the mid-90s we had Geocities

---

[1]Marco Camisani Calzolari, Franco Giacomazzi, *Impresa 4.0. Marketing e comunicazione digitale a 4 direzioni*, Edizioni Pearson - Financial Times 2008.

and TheGlobe.com, which allowed users to set up a web page on a server and interact with people having similar interests.

SixDegrees (1997) marked the advent of social networks as we now know them. It allowed users to create a personal profile and establish online friendships with other people.

In 2002 it was Friendster's turn. With 3 million users in three months of life it inaugurated the golden season of social networks. MySpace deployed the following year and soon became the planet's foremost social network, a position it held until 2007.

Launched in 2004, Facebook is now the most widely used horizontal (i.e., generalist) social network in Europe, the United States, Brazil, Canada, and Australia. It is enormously popular across genders, ages, and social classes, with somewhere in the neighbourhood of one billion registered users.

YouTube, Badoo, LinkedIn, Twitter and others such as V Kontakte and Odnoklassniki (Russia), Orkut (Brazil, India) and Zing (China) are also impressive examples, but Facebook continues to be perceived in the West as the quintessential social network.

A more recent arrival is Google+, the latest offspring of the Google family. Many have hailed it (with all the hype that has become typical of these phenomena) "the new Facebook". It integrates many of the Google web services (gmail, search, YouTube, etc.) into a single social network account. It makes it possible to divide up friends and acquaintances into very specific circles and offers other interesting functionalities such as indexing posts on Google. Launched in 2011, it now has some 200 million users, half of whom are active on a monthly basis.

Rightly or wrongly, social networks are commonly perceived as a revolution. They represent the New that advances, and everyone has to come to terms with them, whether they want to be there or not. (Rest assured, whether you're there or not, someone in there is going to be talking about you.) There are those who trumpet them as the dawn of a new epoch and others who downplay them as a passing fad. Of course, the truth lies somewhere in the middle, but it is not easy to discern.

The mass media help to accentuate this difficulty. In their usual sensationalist and slipshod way, they present these tools as a panacea for every ill and then turn around and cast aspersions on their negative aspects. All this does is exacerbate the anxiety of being left out, of not being where so many say you have to be.

A company without a digital strategy that envisages a presence on one or more social networks is now immediately branded as being out-dated. But are they really? On the other hand, digital agencies are pushing more and more in that direction, offering a myriad of new and exotic professional figures who essentially manage their clients' social network profiles.

To complete the picture, social networks are almost always free of charge. There is a very gentle learning curve, they offer a "democratic" template, with a limited number of things that can be customized, and thus seem to offer everyone the same opportunities.

Within this somewhat confusing framework, where company websites are being cannibalized by the social networks and see their usership waning, many are asking themselves whether it is really worth it to update, transform, or even keep the company website or blog alive. In the era of social networks these sites seem drab, outmoded, and in a word, useless.

Image 1: Which way in?

1.1.2. To Be There or Not To Be There?

So, what to do? If ignoring social networks does not seem to be an option, what choices must be made to successfully manage a modern company? Here's where things can get a bit overwhelming. Open a Facebook page? A Twitter account? A YouTube channel? All three? And then what happens? How come no one watches my videos? Why do I have so few fans and followers? Why don't more people join?

It will not take much searching on the web to find countless websites and blogs bursting with advice from communication and advertising experts (some with dubious credentials) who teach you "how to be social", how to manage a Facebook page, what content to post, how to stimulate one's audience and generate engagement, and how to handle crises if by chance– heaven forbid!– you make a mistake.

Granted the fact that managing a Facebook page is not, and will never be, an exact science, it is true that these media differ profoundly from mass media in the way information moves. It does not ripple outward from a central point to a great multitude of orbiting points (the broadcasting paradigm of radio, television, newspapers, etc.), it is exchanged on a peer basis with others. It is not a monologue but a dialogue. It is of fundamental importance to perceive and understand what is said to us and about us, and it is thus wise to prepare to approach this environment in the best way possible.

Social networks are not the cakewalk they may seem to be. They demand time, dedication, professionalism and constancy– in a word, commitment. The greater the commitment the greater the level of interaction. And interaction with a large audience is exactly what many are after.

It is clear that to manage social profiles the way they should be managed, i.e., with specific results in mind, some sort of financial investment will also be necessary. Exactly what sort will obviously depend on the nature of the company and the objectives its has set forth. We will examine exactly what constitutes the "right" choice for each type of company, depending on its size and objectives, further on (Chapter 3).

After we have registered ourselves on a social network, how do we assess the results? This is another fundamental question. We will also analyse the age-old question of ROI (Return on Investment), an overvalued parameter, and discover that there are no exhaustive and reliable indicators of success.

The aim of this book is to make it clear that social networks are a marketing tool, like the telephone, newsletter or billboards, that the results cannot be measured distinct from the overall strategy, and that measuring the "profits from social media" is a completely nonsensical concept.

The numerical indicators so proudly paraded by these platforms (numbers of fans, number of followers, number of views) are purpose-made to stroke egos, to appeal to our vanity, to stimulate competition and give us a heady illusion of "success". There are also psychological explanations for this phenomenon, and we will look at these too further on. What needs to be said here is that if, as a company, I decide to open a fanpage with the sole purpose of accumulating the greatest possible number of fans, there is hardly any point in opening it. Numbers are important, but they are perhaps the most overrated indicator of all when we are talking about success on social networks. The time when journalists were dazzled by those numbers and blazoned them on the front page is over. Figures relating to the digital world are sterile and useless without a solid strategy behind them. It is roughly the equivalent of wanting to assemble a large crowd in a specific place and then not knowing what to say to them or where to take them from there.

1.1.3. The Miracles of Facebook

There is a lot of confusion regarding the role of Facebook or other social networks in marketing. Nearly magical virtues have been attributed to social media marketing in the recent period, to the point where it now appears to be the principal digital marketing approach used by companies. Facebook in particular promises great things, things that are nearly unimaginable with traditional media channels. Does it not boast close to a billion users? Is it not the world's second largest nation by population? How can you imagine not being part of it, not being in touch with such a large part of the market?

These are legitimate concerns, but they immediately summon forth at least two observations. One is that it is not always necessary for a company to reach the entire world; it might be better to concentrate on a specific market niche, even just on the local level.

The second observation regards a misunderstanding of the nature of these new media. Not being mechanisms for broadcasting– but rather narrowcasting, podcasting and "niche-casting"– a message communicated on these networks does not simultaneously reach all the users of a platform such as Facebook. I remember an anecdote about a journalist who wrote a few years ago (but not so many): "You jump out of a window so you can end up on YouTube". He clearly lumps YouTube in the same camp as television, where "ending up" means creating a sensation. But what he misses is the fact that all it takes to end up on

YouTube– for anyone, himself included– is simply to upload a video!

Something that relates to the allure of "large numbers of users" is the reasoning of those who think that their advertising will have enormous visibility and that their posts will reach all of their fans. I really hate to break your hearts, but you're going to have to stop dreaming.

Another common illusion is that if we manage to win our customers' sympathies (anything but easy), they will become our champions and further our cause, promoting our brand for free. That is really far-fetched. The truth of the matter is that Facebook is not a platform that was invented to be a showcase for brands, it was invented to allow people to communicate. And what's more, people on Facebook are generally not interested in following brands, and much less keen on talking about them (except perhaps to trash them).

One of the main tasks here is to cut through the illusions and grasp the fact, right from the start, that social networks are not an easy-catch fish farm with a teeming pond stocked with customers ready to take the bait as soon as you cast your line. In order to reel in their true bounty, to gain the maximum benefit, you have to understand their true nature, their true potential, and their true limitations.

1.1.4. The Company Website: The Backbone

Is it really necessary to maintain the company website? Who is going to visit it? How can it possibly compete with the millions of attractions on Facebook?

These are very pertinent questions and there are many who ask them. Before we start looking at answers, let us pose a simple question: "What would happen if Facebook were to disappear tomorrow?"

Absurd? I'm not so sure. The eventuality is well within the realm of the possible. The web evolves quickly, the next big thing is just around the corner. Facebook is already suffering the erosive effects of niche networks (vertical networks) and people and companies are beginning to show signs of tiring of it. It has been a flop on the stock market and has yet to show a clear strategy for the future.

Social networks are not going to die out, Facebook may well endure, but it could undergo deep transformation. Actually this is already happening. We are powerless in the face of change, and we are subject to the decisions of others. It's obvious: the platform does not belong to us, it belongs to Facebook! And as soon as you upload content, that becomes Facebook's property too. And if Facebook changes its rules? For example, if it decides to make us pay for every "like" we receive? Or maybe to get access to a business account?

You may think: But the customers are mine! Wrong. Because if you only use Facebook, you actually know almost nothing about your customers. You only know as much as Facebook lets you know.

We will come back to this issue in depth. But in the meantime, what answer would you give to this question: where do you think a customer who wants to buy something from you is going to go? To your Facebook page or to the company website?

It has been shown (Incyte Group and Get Satisfaction[2]) that people looking for information to guide their purchasing decisions prefer to consult the brand website, which is perceived as being more trustworthy and accurate than a Facebook page. And when they make the actual purchase, customers tend to prefer stores on websites– indeed, many prominent Facebook stores quite quickly fizzled out.

A major study by the Incyte Group with the sponsorship of Get Satisfaction redefines the importance of having a private (branded) community. Below we present some excerpts.

---

[2] Get Satisfaction e Incyte Group,
http://info.getsatisfaction.com/rs/getsatisfaction/images/IncyteGroup_Whitepaper_Q3 2012.pdf.

To Monetize Open Social Networks, Invite Customers to Be More Than Just "Friends"
(Get Satisfaction - Incyte Group)

The Methodology

For this study[3], Incyte's research team surveyed thousands of U.S. consumers to identify demographic information, their understanding and use of Internet technology, and their use of open social networks. In addition, the survey included conjoint analytic techniques to understand their preferences around branded customer communities, including:
- The value propositions that would attract them
- How they preferred to learn about these communities
- The role of the sponsoring brand;
- The extent of social media linkages they would like to see.

The results focused on responses from 1,897 qualified consumers who actively use the Internet and represent adults from all age, socio-economic, and geographic groups in the U.S.

---

[3] http://info.getsatisfaction.com/rs/getsatisfaction/images/IncyteGroup_Whitepaper_Q32012.pdf

"We were able to build a model of consumer preferences for the entire U.S. adult population of Internet users," notes Sakai. "This model allows us [...] to build a very robust picture of the features and contexts that will drive consumers to join these communities."

Open Social Network Characteristics	Branded Customer Community Characteristics
• Examples: Facebook, Twitter, blogs • Designed as a social experience to primarily connect people to people around similar interests • Brands may or may not participate, but only have a limited ability to manage the community or vet its content • Supports social sharing between individuals • Trust is based on personal relationships	• Examples: Ask Pampers, Mint.com Customer Community • Designed as a customer engagement community to connect people to people and people to companies • Brands proactively manage the community and control content • Supports social sharing between individuals, the company, and advocates • Trust is based on reputation of the participants, which is measured by the perceived value of their social media content and participation levels

Image 2: Main differences between open social networks and branded communities.

Key Findings

1. Social networks are not the first place people go to research products and services. Google and brand websites are.

Facebook, Twitter, and other open social networks are not necessarily where consumers go to build relationship with companies or learn about and evaluate products and services.

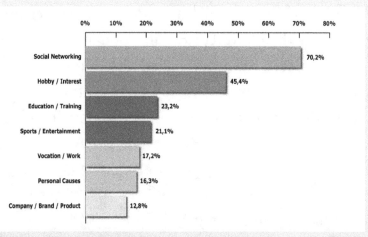

Image 3: Primary Reasons Consumers Use Social Networks

As shown in Image 3, they primarily want to use these sites to connect with friends and family and pursue personal interests; only 12.8% use them to research brands and product details.

Company Websites are still the primary destinations for information to support a purchase decision. As shown in Image 4, when Incyte asked participants to name their primary destinations for researching products or seeking customer service via the Internet, their top choices were:

- Visit company Website to make a purchase decision – 89.3%

- Visit company Website for service/support questions – 68.8%
- Contact the company via email – 43.5%
- Use an Internet community dedicated to the product/service – 27.3%
- Use a social network – 21.2%

[...] there is an opportunity here for companies to create branded customer communities specifically dedicated to these consumer goals – communities that are part of the website experience that supports the brand.

2: Consumers showed a strong preference for branded customer communities over open social networks for building relationships with brands.

When people are introduced to a new product, service, or brand through a social network and want to learn more about it, 81.1% said they would first visit the company Website, and 25.7% would visit a retail store. Only 19% would look at its Facebook page.

This further validates that consumers do not expect to find detailed information about products and services on open social networks. Rather, these sites are where people are more likely to begin to look for relevant products or services, or to discover them through a friend.

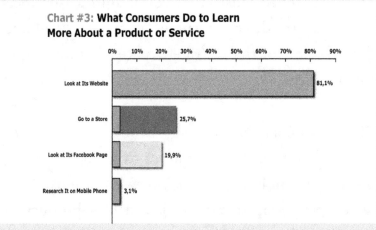

Image 4: What consumers do to learn more about a product or service

Considered separately, these last two findings may seem paradoxical; but when looked at within the broader context of the study, they make perfect sense.

3. Consumers don't want brand relationships to be a part of their open social networks; instead, they want company Websites to be more like their experiences with open social networks.

This way, they get the best of both worlds when researching new products and services – specifically, detailed product information from the company and real-life answers and opinions from other customers. They do not want their social networks to become corporate experiences.

Characteristics of Branded Community Experiences Preferred by Consumers:

• Managed by the company
• Linked with social networks, integrated with the company's Website, and indexed by search engines
• Providing detailed content that is relevant to members' changing context (shopper, new user seeking service or technical assistance, etc.)
• Providing a community member profile with user reputation data to help them assess the trustworthiness of peer answers and comments
• Ideally integrated with the company's e-commerce Website so shoppers can easily view social conversa-

tions and opinions as they research products.

http://info.getsatisfaction.com/rs/getsatisfaction/images/I
ncyteGroup_Whitepaper_Q32012.pdf

These results are in line with those of a recent study by Duepuntozero Research and Connexia[4]. According to the study, 8 million Italians regularly participate in communities associated with specific brands or companies and a million and a half visit those communities every day. With a branded community, 81% of consumers say they are better informed about products and initiatives, as opposed to 71% on Facebook. If 65% of the members of a brand community say they consume more of the company's products (as opposed to 55% for Facebook), the importance of the branded community becomes very real.

Communities dedicated specifically to a brand are generally more capable of attracting "true" fans than are their Facebook equivalents. Only 26% of adherents to a Facebook brand page say they are actually a fan and a consumer of the brand, as opposed to 32% of those in a branded community. In both cases, contests and promotions seem to be a strong factor in increasing membership.

Keeping the company (or self owned) website alive and nourished means occupying an environment free of extern-

---

[4] http://www.mymarketing.it/dblog/articolo.asp?articolo=1587.

ally imposed limits where the content is our own property and visitors can be tracked and profiled as we like. The role of the social networks is to channel people to our shores. And it will be very beneficial if the users find something to match their expectations when they get there.

1.2. The Miraculous Rise of Social Media Marketing

Image 5: An infinite chain of opportunity

1.2.1. Have Social Networks Killed Off Blogs and Websites?

How are company websites faring in the era of Facebook? Do people still visit them? Who?

The data is not encouraging. Website traffic is declining all over the world. Why? Before we get to this question, let us have a quick overview of the history of company websites.

In the days of Web 1.0, many companies set up a company website. More often than not they were static, difficult to find, and difficult to use, often having been created by web agencies with little real expertise. Initial publicity consisted of banners. The goal was to develop a high level of "stickiness", i.e., the amount of time a user remained on the website.

With the advent of the social web, Web 2.0 (an outdated, threadbare term that I can hardly bear to utter anymore), many companies upgraded their websites with blogs that were often quite interesting and popular among followers. But that was nearly ten years ago.

The stage was set for the debut of the new social networks. As we will see in the next section, after some initial hesitation, companies started flocking to these new frontiers *en masse*, lured partially by the evangelical work of social gurus.

With the advent of social media, much of the traffic that had earlier circulated in the blogosphere was absorbed by the new media and there was even talk of the "end of the blog". In effect, many blogs languished and withered as their owners discovered social networks. For this portion of bloggers, whose blogs were just a means for satisfying their desires for sharing and socializing, the shift to social networks was natural, it represented a valid and much simpler alternative.

I remember that the term "blogger" lived on to define those who post interesting content online that attracts a fair number of followers. In other words, the term blogger has come to refer to the activity, not to the medium.

Blogs remain quite significant among the various means used by bloggers and thus it would be a serious mistake to shut down company blogs, as Ducati Italia did in 2010. Here is their good-bye message[5] and the announcement of their rebirth on Facebook:

"Progress and online tools move forward quickly and we always seek to keep in step with the times. And so we have decided to close our Desmoblog so that we can focus all our efforts on other conversation spaces.

---

[5] http://blog.ducati.com/post/260/arrivederci-2.

"As you know, some time ago we opened a Facebook page. It is an open space, and it is accessible also to those who are not registered Facebook users. Over 180,000 have chosen it as a way of staying in touch with us. We also dialogue with motorcycle lovers and the online media through Twitter, and we use our YouTube channel to show you some fun and (we hope!) interesting videos."

Some studies (such as the *Webtrends*[6] study, quoted extensively in the box below) have effectively shown that the increasing traffic on Facebook has absorbed much of the usership of company websites. Over the 12 months of the study, visits to most of the websites of the Fortune top 100 companies were stagnant or declining. A full 68% recorded negative growth, with an average drop of 24% in unique visitors.

The study examined 44 websites, half of which offer e-commerce options. The fact that some 40% of the monitored companies recorded more traffic on their fanpage than on their website makes one stop and think.

---

[6] *Research: Success of Social Commerce,*
http://webtrends.com/shared/whitepaper/Whitepaper-SuccessOfSocialCommerce-Webtrends.pdf.

The Effect of Social Networks and the Mobile Web on Website Traffic and the Inevitable Rise of Facebook Commerce
(Webtrends.com)

There is a popular perception that brand websites are losing traffic to their Facebook counterparts.

As a step towards finding quantitative evidence, we analyzed the website traffic of Fortune 100 websites based on 'unique visits'.

The study revealed that 68% of the top 100 companies were experiencing a negative growth in unique visits over the past year, with an average drop of 23%.

To ascertain if Facebook had a part to play in this decline, unique visits to a brand's website were compared with unique visits to its Facebook page (obtained using fan count as a proxy) within a three to five month period. In a sample of 44 companies, 40% exhibited higher traffic to their Facebook page compared to their website. When these companies were categorized based on the presence or absence of e-Commerce transactions, we found that the majority of the companies (65%) in the 'Non e-Commerce' category received higher traffic on Facebook compared to their website. On the other hand, most companies (about 77%) featuring e-commerce did vastly better on their websites, although exhibiting a sharp decline in annual visits.

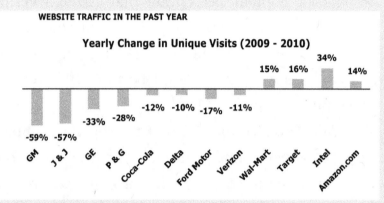

Image 6: Yearly change in unique visits

[...] With the mobile web growing in size and popularity, it is time for brands and retailers to understand that surviving online is no longer about all-in-one websites, but measuring and improving performance in all the social, mobile and web entities. To test the hypothesis of decreasing website traffic, we analyzed the one year (Nov 2009 – Nov 2010) traffic trend of the top 100 Fortune 500 companies. The number of unique visitors to websites was obtained from Compete.com and the percentage decrease/increase calculated.

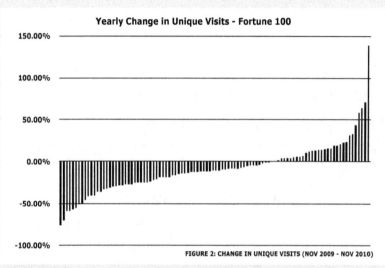

Image 7: yearly change in unique visits

Website vs. Facebook traffic comparison

The next step in our research was to understand if Facebook played a role in the declining visits to websites.

Research Methodology

Unique visits to a brand's website were taken from Compete.com for Aug and Nov 2010. The difference between these two data points gave the increase/decrease in the number of unique visitors to a website over a three month period. Since publicly available data for Facebook statistics is very limited, fan count was used as a proxy for unique visits. The number of fans for a brand's page was noted in Aug 2010 and Jan 2011. The difference between these two numbers is the number of newly added fans in a five month period. This number represented only a fraction of the unique visitors because it did not account for: old fans would have visited again; or visitors who would have left without becoming a fan, etc.

Thus, the number of newly added fans represented the minimum increase in unique visitors that can be assumed for a Facebook page – a lowball figure. In this respect our analysis grossly underestimates the potential of Facebook. Even though the period of data collection is in favor of Facebook (five months compared to three months for websites), we feel it does not skew the results as it is well compensated by the lower estimates used as proxies. Finally, companies were grouped into two categories: 'e-Commerce' and 'Non e-Commerce' based on whether their websites supported e-Commerce transactions. A sample of 22 companies was selected in each of the two categories bringing the test sample up to 44.

Findings

• Among the 44 companies, 18 companies (about 40%) exhibited extremely high traffic to their Facebook page compared to their websites. Not only were their websites accounting for fewer unique visits than Facebook, but many were also showing a decline in visits over the three month period.

• Of the 22 categorized as 'Non-e-Commerce', 13 companies (about 65%) received more unique visits to their Facebook page compared to their website (Image 8)

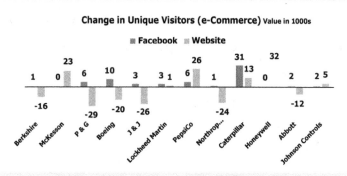

Image 8: change in unique visitors (non e-Commerce)

Two companies that exhibited extremely high Facebook traffic were Coca-Cola and Walt Disney (Image 9).

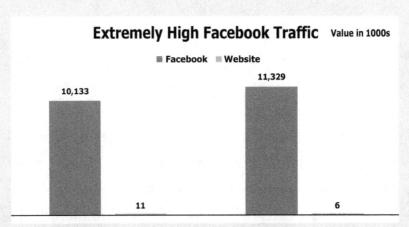

Image 9: Extremely high Facebook traffic

• Of the 22 companies having e-Commerce transactions, only five exhibited promising Facebook trends, while the rest (about 77%) portrayed very consistent traffic to their websites (Image 10).

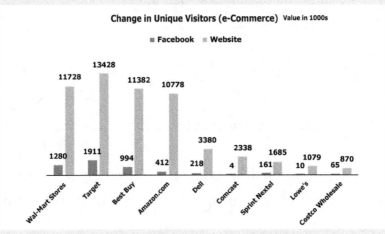

Image 10: Change in unique visitors (e-Commerce)

Even though these websites fare better than Facebook currently, their future growth is questionable since many have started to experience significant drops in unique visits compared to last year.

Is e-commerce a short-lived protection for websites?

The striking contrast in traffic trends among websites in the categories discussed above indicates that e-Commerce may be one of the factors protecting websites from the influence of Facebook. What would happen if Facebook begins to provide a seamless e-commerce experience?

To answer this, we looked at Delta Airlines which recently enabled customers to book tickets right on its Facebook page. On a year-over-year basis, Delta is experiencing a 9.53% drop in unique visitors to its website. While Delta's website lost more than a million unique visitors over a three month period, its Facebook page gained more than a 1000 new fans. Although this single instance is not sufficient evidence to conclude, it is an early sign of declining website popularity in the future.

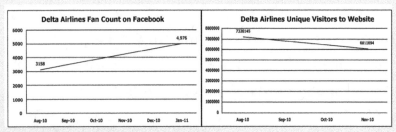

Image 11: High Facebook traffic

Mobile web

It is not the social network alone that is threatening brand websites. The mobile web is also contending for a big piece of the "traffic pie" and has reached exponential growth before we realized the magnitude of its footprint. [...]

But recent reports from PayPal indicate that there was a 300% increase in mobile shopping and payments during the 2010 holiday season, which signifies a big wave of behavioral change that is sweeping the shopping community. The trend does not go unnoticed by online retailers. According to a dotMobi report, the number of mobile-ready websites grew from 150,000 in 2008 to 3,000,000 in 2010 (an increase of 2000%).

The analysts at Morgan Stanley predict that in five years the number of people accessing the web via mobile devices will surpass those accessing it from desktops. These statistics are backed by reports from Quantcast that mobile web usage increased by 110% from 2008 to 2009 and continues to exhibit exponential growth.

http://webtrends.com/shared/whitepaper/Whitepaper-SuccessOfSocialCommerce-Webtrends.pdf

In a post commenting on this study[7], Jeff Bullas highlights traffic on the websites of three food giants:

Coca Cola: -40% in just 12 months;

Starbucks: stagnant;

Nabisco: -74% in one year (from 1.2 million visits a month to 321,000).

Comparing these to their fans on Facebook:

Coca Cola: 22 million fans on Facebook

Starbucks: 19 million

Oreo: 8 million

Given all that, it is perfectly reasonable to wonder whether it is worthwhile maintaining the company website, or if it is doomed to disappear over the course of a few years. Will users still visit the websites or will they limit themselves to Facebook and related apps to check news, products, promotions, etc.?

---

[7] Is Facebook killing off the company website?
http://www.jeffbullas.com/2011/03/21/is-facebook-killing-off-the-company-website.

In my opinion, we mustn't mix user desire to socialize on platforms such as Facebook into the decision to maintain or close the company website. The defection of users noted above is due mainly to the low quality of the websites. As we know, in most cases we are talking about static websites based on Adobe Flash offering large and cumbersome PDF files for downloading and rife with other problems. They cannot possibly compare to the agility of media like Facebook, which is endowed with the latest technologies such as Ajax, are updated in real time with content changing before your eyes, and allow interaction at all levels with people who share your interests, not unlike what you might find in the neighbourhood sports bar.

If company websites continue to be made this way, they cannot expect anything better than what is described above in the box. In Chapter 3 we will look at some concrete cases representing a completely different idea of websites, with quite different results in terms of traffic. I can state with total confidence that the crisis is due solely to the absence of sufficient attractions for a modern user. When the proper investment is made both in communication strategy and technology, the results are profoundly different, and demonstrate that a branded website has a reason for existing and can generate more profit, in both the middle and the long term, than social networks belonging to third parties.

1.2.2. The Birth of the Super Guru 2.0

Image 12: An impeccable Curriculum Vitae

How has social media marketing become so important? Why is it proposed by hundreds of web agencies and often sought out as a first resort by companies?

It will help to quickly review the history of the web and digital agencies to get an understanding of this.

In the beginning, these agencies were called web agencies. Their services included the creation and implementation of websites. These were the days of Web 1.0. There was no such thing as a digital strategy per se; a company opened a website because that is what it had to do, and that was all there was to it.

In 2001-2004, with the bursting of the new economy bubble, the spread of digital came to a standstill. Companies appeared to lose interest in the web in those years.

But the web was changing in the meantime. And far from fading out, as was imagined, it transformed, acquiring a completely new social dimension. The architectural technology changed. With the development of services that could be accessed via web, use became more active and contributive, providing the basis for user-generated content. The transition from html to dhtml (dynamic html) allowed interaction with website content in real time. Furthermore, the number of people connected to the internet had greatly increased.

Digital culture pundits (myself included) began talking about what was going on. We illustrated the trends underway on the web, the flourishing of blogs, the importance of listening to users and establishing a dialogue, and so on. We prepared the ground for the great leap in the dark: from the desert to the social web. Second Life was the first to arrive in that period, followed by Facebook, and suddenly the agencies realized that it was no longer necessary to worry about the technical aspects, which had become increasingly complex, but that it was enough to convince companies to open a simple Facebook account. Anyone can write a book– I have– but it takes a lot more to put a man on the moon. In the first case it is enough to assemble a large number of words and advice of some arguable value. In the other, you need tens of thousands of people at the highest level of specialization, with a great degree of team coordination because activities requiring an extensive technological basis demand very high capability levels.

As demand for digital increased enormously, supply responded to meet it. In other words, anyone could easily reinvent themselves as a social media guru without having to assemble a NASA-scale team.

For companies it seemed too good to be true: no more expensive websites to set up and maintain, all it took was the small effort of opening a free Facebook page and put an underpaid intern in charge of managing it.

On the other hand there were numbers, grand numbers. The dazzling growth of platforms such as MySpace, YouTube, and Facebook gave many the impression that the market was undergoing powerful development. The illusion was boosted by an old and misguided conception of the mass audience. The thought was: "If YouTube has millions of users, millions of people will see my video", just as what happens with a primetime television commercial during the Superbowl.

And so social media marketing and internet PR agencies sprang up like mushrooms. And with them came a host of new and "indispensable" professionals: the Social Media Manager, the Community Manager, the Social Influencer, the Social Marketing Manager, the Digital PR Specialist, the Positioning Manager and the Contextual Prospect Advertiser, as well as the Social Disseminator, Posting Expert and absolutely vital Fan Moderation Manager. And of course behind these exotic figures was a whole business of schools and para-schools to train them, for a few thousand euros.

It won't escape you that these high sounding names are not backed up by well defined professional roles. There can be no question that many of these roles are improvised and offer little real substance. Furthermore, many of these social media gurus lack the proper marketing experience, while vice versa, many marketeers do not have a very good grasp on social media.

And so we have created a dialogue among the deaf, leading to strategies with little hope of success, including, as we will see below, the acquisition of fake fans and fake followers, which are necessary to perpetuate the myth of the value of a large audience.

1.2.3. You are the Influencer!

With the advent of Internet PR agencies, the concept of influencer also began to be bandied about. Influencers are people who companies see as being capable of influencing the opinions of broad swaths of the population. These influencers are not so much people who are influential offline as well (singers, sports stars, etc.) who receive generous recompense for promoting products to their large audiences of fans. An influencer, in general, is someone who has built up influence on the web. They are considered to be experts. They almost always have very popular blogs. They get a lot of "likes" on Facebook, many retweets, and lots of shares. Their opinions are considered to be beyond manipulation. They are able to influence purchasing decisions, voting decisions, and more. In short, they are manna from heaven for those working in PR and non-conventional marketing.

But do influencers really exist?

I am rather sceptical on this question. Some consider me to be one, but I do not think so, at least not in the most common sense of the term. I have a hard enough time influencing my eight-year-old son, let alone thousands of people.

Many are sceptical of the real influence of these figures. Each of us, on the internet as in life, has his or her own audience and some amount of influence. Are we all influencers? Or is nobody one?

In any case, if influencers do exist, there must be some way to measure their influence. And indeed there are a number of different online influence measurers, among which Klout is the best known and most widely used.

Klout assigns an influence score on a scale from 0 to 100. It is based on the quantity of reactions or interactions that a subject causes on various social platforms. Klout has aroused a great deal of criticism because it uses a secret and– worse yet– easily spoofed algorithm. For example, it takes into consideration the number of mentions on Twitter. Hence, to get a higher score all it takes is for influencers to greet each other every day (people with high Klout scores are obviously worth more).

And other problems have not been lacking. In July 2012, while the algorithm was being revised, many so-called influencers all saw their scores reduced to 10. Imagine their humiliation.

Now Klout has decided to perfect its algorithm (and while they're at it, give a facelift to their graphics). As explained by Joe Fernandez, Klout CEO, the algorithm will now take into account 400 signals instead of 100. It will include mentions on Facebook, likes, comments, sub-scribers and updates. For Twitter it will count retweets, quotes, followers, responses. On Google+ it will count +1s, reshares and comments, and also LinkedIn connections, comments, and recommendations, Foursquare suggestions, +K received, and citations on Wikipedia.

The only possible comment: imagining you can measure something intangible (and non-definable) such as the influence of one person on other people is an error of methodology. Indeed, Klout is based on analytics provided by social media that are crude and of little significance. Let's take for example a parameter such as sharing. If I share some content it doesn't necessarily mean that the person I got it from influences me.

The mechanism of virality is the classic example of sharing content that does not derive from the influence of the person who shares it. Indeed, content posted by complete unknowns has been known to go viral. Nevertheless, the obsession for quantities and dimensions is difficult to shake. Especially when even the iPhone is longer than it used to be.

1.2.4. The Hype Cycle Fever

Another thing contributing to the feeling that "being on social networks" is indispensable is the general public consensus, as always picked up and amplified by traditional media for their own ends.

The story of the relationship between old media and the internet is well known. These communication channels are fascinated by this network. They address the theme with increasing frequency, but unfortunately tend to seek out its sensationalistic aspects rather than examine the issues with due rigour. An example from a few years ago is Second Life, a platform comprising an online role-playing game (Multi-User Dungeon – MUD), proposing a virtual world that seeks to mimic our own.

Second Life was presented by both journalists and the super gurus with an emphasis on its emotional, evocative or scandalous aspects, using ultra-high definition fluid images. The reality was different: on most computers, a person's avatar jerked along ever so slowly. But Second Life fever infected companies and agencies. They sold virtual spaces in that world, operations that created a great hoopla in the media. Two years later both Second Life and the islands had disappeared, and along with them their supporters. The only winners were the web agencies who had sold the islands.

Image 13: May 1, 2006 Cover of Business Week

More recently, the phenomenon has touched Twitter and Pinterest, the rising star of social media.

The media influence expectations and inflate the importance of new technologies, including social networks, but then they also tear them down using an equally sensationalist approach. This is part of a phenomenon known as the *hype cycle*.

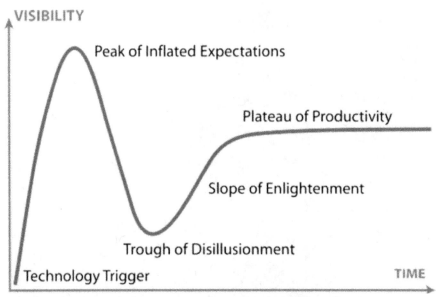

Image 14: Hype Cycle - For each new technology, after an initial peak of enthusiasm, there is a collapse of expectations before a relatively stable plateau of productivity is reached.

The thing that is important to note is that it is very important to develop your own critical faculties. Most of the time that someone, speaking about the web, tries to convince you of something, they will resort to hyperbole in one sense or another. Myself included!

1.3. Facebook Tools for Companies

"Ask not what your company can do on Facebook; ask what Facebook can do for your company."

1.3.1. A Comedy of Fanpage Errors

A fanpage is the equivalent of a personal profile page but dedicated to companies, celebrities, organizations of all sorts, and animals. If your dog has her own personal page, you should advise her to open a fanpage. If she doesn't understand, call a social media guru to explain it to her for you.

A user becomes a fan by liking the fanpage. From then on, he can access the content published on the page and receive updates on his home feed.

Creating a fanpage is a cinch. For that matter, one of the great appeals of Facebook is its usability, counterbalanced by rather limited possibilities for personalization. You can post all sorts of content on the fanpage– external links, images, videos– just as with a normal user profile.

Fanpages are public, and thus indexed by search engines.

Image 15: A smooth path to success?

The tool for user flow monitoring on the fanpage is provided by Facebook and is called Facebook Insights. It uses a series of parameters (Reach, Engaged User, People Talking About This, etc.) and aggregated data to give us an idea of what sort of audience we have (by age, sex, etc.). Armed with this knowledge, we are better able to tailor our posted content to suit them and thus boost our success.

Once you create the fanpage, you have to populate and manage it. This is where all sorts of errors are often made. As I said above, there is already a great deal of guidance in the literature. And how could it be otherwise, given the rise of new sorts of professionals, such as the Facebook Page Creator, whose purpose is to manage Facebook pages?

Although this is not really pertinent to the purpose of this book, I will give you a quick overview of some of the most common and egregious errors:

- Flooding similar pages or groups with spam to call attention to your own page. As well as being a time consuming activity, there is no return to be had and it is also risky– Facebook might perk up its ears and close your account;

- Addressing fans using inappropriate language: dull, sloppy, ungrammatical, politically incorrect, etc.;

- Posting with inappropriate frequency, either not often enough or too often (and ending up being seen as a royal pain);

- Not making clear links to your own website (error of errors!) or using an image that is not coordinated with your website;

- Not knowing how to respond appropriately to criticism and attacks by your fans, triggering a crisis.

Nevertheless, the fanpage can be used precisely to fulfil the ends suggested by this book (see Chapter 3), i.e., as a source of traffic. Users gather around the page in an organic fashion (i.e., without you having invested money in assembling and grouping them) and are channelled in specific ways to sites belonging to the company.

Recently, Facebook identified fanpages as a great source of income and began to put a price on their most important functions, such as Reach. In practical terms, the more you pay, the more your fans will see what you write. Those who invested a great deal of energy in recent years populating their fanpage with large numbers of fans, only to find that now they can only interact with a small percentage of them, obviously made the wrong choice. Those who invested in more farsighted strategies, on the other hand, may now enjoy an unmediated relationship with their fans.

1.3.2. Pay to Be Seen: publicity on Facebook

"Social network companies have been forced to disguise new advertising models (for example, sponsored tweets or Facebook ads) as real consumer advocacy."
Dale Sakai, partner, The Incyte Group

Investing in an advertising campaign on Facebook may serve to call attention to a company's fanpage and cause it to be populated, as well as to publicize the company's own website (although, as we will see, it is not very effective at doing so). In any case, one of the most mistaken lines of reasoning is: "How much do I have to invest to reach n fans?" I will repeat *ad nauseam* that the goal must not be to reach n fans, but to use Facebook to find new customers. Customers are better than fans. So, it's great if the fanpage is populated, but there has to be something interesting on it, and that something has to be clearly linked to the company website. Only after having grasped this, and thus the importance of a solid strategy, does it make sense to consider making well-calculated investments.

In order to become an advertiser, all you have to do is be a registered Facebook user with a normal user profile, or else with an advertising account. A company that decides to launch an advertising campaign on Facebook may then choose among:

- Simple Ads
- Sponsored Stories
- Facebook Offers
- Promoted Posts

While the simple ad is the most classic form, sponsored stories exploit Facebook's social potential, showing things that our friends like and encouraging us to do the same.

Facebook Offers are like coupons. If you click on them you receive an email (from Facebook, not from the company, and thus at the address you provided to FB when you registered) with a discount coupon.

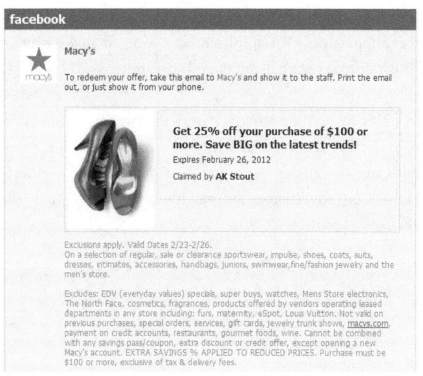

Image 16: Facebook Offer

Promoted Posts are simple posts created on the fanpage. The difference is that we pay for them, to the delight of

Facebook. The algorithm that regulates visibility on Facebook (EdgeRank) makes it so each post on a page is seen by an average of 17% of its fans. Thus, by promoting the post, at a cost, you can be sure it will be seen by higher and higher percentages of your fans.

The different sorts of publicity are summarized below:

Type of publicity	What it promotes	What it is	Who sees it
Simple Ad	Fanpage Single post External website	Link Description Image	Everyone (Home- right column on profile)
Sponsored Story	"Likes" for pages and posts Check-ins on page	Heading Description Image Social actions (e.g., Mario Rossi likes "Page X")	Fans of the page and their friends (Home- right column on profile)
Facebook Offer	Special offer (with a discount coupon)	Link Description Image "Send offer" button	Fans of the page and their friends (Home- home feed)
Promoted Post	A post on the fanpage	Post	Fans of the page (Home- home feed)

Image 17: Summary of advertising options on Facebook

Facebook offers the possibility to target a specific audience. On the campaign creation panel it is possible to target users by category (geographical location, demographic data, interests, education, occupation, sentimental status, etc.)

There are two payment methods:

- CPC (Cost Per Click): the advertiser pays every time someone clicks their ad;
- CPM (Cost Per Mille): the advertiser pays for every one thousand views (not clicks).

How much you pay depends on how long the campaign runs and what type of ad is used, but in general, a reasonable rate is €0.23 per click or €0.06 for every thousand views.

1.3.3. Facebook Apps

Facebook apps are programs developed by third parties that only run on Facebook. They integrate into the platform to perform various operations without requiring the user to leave Facebook. They are highly important tools with viral visibility: they are often based on invite-your-friends mechanisms. The most popular apps are video games, but there are also others in e-commerce, such as Ticketmaster, which we will examine in Chapter 3.

1.3.4. The Power of Open Graph

Facebook Open Graph is an API protocol (Application Programming Interface) that allows websites to extract information on people, photos, events, web pages and other objects, as well as the interrelations among them.

Companies can persuade people to use Facebook apps to obtain this information. The exchange of value lies in the fact that these applications require authorization not only to run, but to automatically publish (or share) the interaction with the app with all your friends on Facebook.

Image 18: Tautologies

Open Graph increases quality traffic toward branded websites much more than fans do.

In Chapter 3 we will see some examples of how the Open Graph protocol can be integrated profitably into the Back Home Strategy.

Chapter 2
The Moment of Truth

2.1. The Show is Sold Out but the Audience is Bored

2.1.1. Facebook is not Free!

Like many online services, Facebook only appears to be free of cost. The fact that users can register for free does not mean that Facebook does not make money off its users. It does so by means of advertising and user data.

As you know, when you register for Facebook you have to provide a certain amount of information: name, surname, email address, sex, and age. Facebook encourages us to use our real names and to make sure other information is accurate so that our friends can find us. And they use the same lever in asking us to include a personal photo and to specify our interests, occupational history, the schools we attended, etc. The idea is that it will make it easier for our former co-workers and university classmates to find us.

Facebook's success derives precisely from having enticed people into providing all this information. It has succeeded, in part, by playing on our vanity: we all use Facebook as a showcase, trying to look as good as we can. There is always a very strong temptation to show others just how well we are doing. Thus people who are normally reserved or easily irritated by someone prying into their business offer up their personal information without thinking twice.

With the introduction of the Timeline, and betting on users' inclination to show off, Facebook is shooting for an extremely ambitious objective: have us compile a general summary of our lives, from our births to the present, complete with significant moments, memories, successes, failures (some people like to cry in public), and anything else we might feel like sharing.

What does Facebook do with all this information? It uses it, and in the full light of day. All you need to do is review the privacy policy to realize that Facebook uses all the data we provide and even more: it aggregates this data with that of our friends and with other independently obtained information, such as our geographical position (using GPS).

Image 19: Facebook is free, you fetch a good price.

Image 20: What's better, your privacy or being able to use a Facebook app? (joyoftech.com)

"Your information[1]: Your information is the information that's required when you sign up for the site, as well as the information you choose to share. [...] Your birthday allows us to do things like show you age-appropriate content and advertisements [...]

---

[1] Facebook privacy policy, Facebook.com.

Sometimes we get data from our advertising partners, customers and other third parties that helps us (or them) deliver ads, understand online activity, and generally make Facebook better. For example, **an advertiser may tell us information about you** (like how you responded to an ad on Facebook or **on another site**) in order to measure the effectiveness of– and improve the quality of– ads.

"[...] We also put together data from the information we already have about you and your friends. For example, we may put together data about you to determine which friends we should show you in your News Feed or suggest you tag in the photos you post. We may put together your current city with GPS and other location information we have about you to, for example, tell you and your friends about people or events nearby, or offer deals to you that you might be interested in. We may also put together data about you **to serve you ads** that might be more relevant to you." (Facebook.com)

A key passage in Facebook's Data Use Policy states:

"While you are allowing us to use the information we receive about you, **you always own all of your information.** Your trust is important to us, which is why we don't share information we receive about you with others unless we have received your permission; given you notice, such as by telling you about it in this policy; or removed your name or any other personally identifying information from it."

We are the owners of our information. However, Facebook uses it and makes money from it. That's the deal, it's all above board. The data belongs to the user but may be used, with the user's consent, for the business pursuits of third parties. The fact that the user accepts this policy authorizes Facebook to withhold this data from third parties. But some of those third parties are companies that mistakenly think they have hauled in a bounty of information on fans with their fanpage-snares.

Image 21: Zuckerberg

If I have a fanpage I can see who my fans are and the information that they have decided to make public. Most of the data is aggregated. The email address is not part of it, and even if it is visible, it cannot be exported. However, in an attempt to defend itself against accusations of teasing advertisers without delivering the dope (the information, of course), Facebook has formally offered the option of allowing companies to export their fans' email addresses when backing up their page. But this will only work for fans who have edited their privacy settings to allow it. Not many do.

In May the company made its debut on the stock exchange with an extremely high initial offer, 180 billion dollars. But it flopped in just a few months. According to some, the reason is simply because it "sells" something it doesn't own. And the investors are not completely convinced.

2.1.2. I don't want to be friends with my butter!

What is the attitude of Facebook users toward brands and fanpages? You won't like this, but they really don't care much about you or your company, at least while they are on Facebook.

Image 22: Fun on the farm.

As we saw in Chapter 1, many studies, including one recently published[2] (July 2012) by Get Satisfaction and Incyte, show that 70% of people log on to Facebook to network with their friends and family:

Fewer than 13% say they use social media to interact with companies, brands, or products. The attitude of people on Facebook is similar to that of patrons enjoying an aperitif at a bar. They are there to get away from it all,

---

[2] Get Satisfaction e Incyte,
http://info.getsatisfaction.com/rs/getsatisfaction/images/IncyteGroup_Whitepaper_Q3 2012.pdf.

to have fun, to show off, and seek human warmth, communicate with people dear to them– they certainly don't want to listen to promotional messages. I am sure that not one of the almost one billion Facebook users signed up thinking, "Wow! Now I can become a fan of Coca-Cola!" And yet people do become fans of the brand. Why?

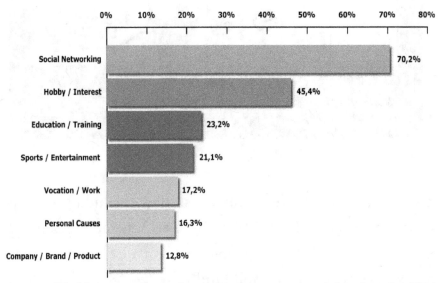

Image 23: Main reasons why consumers use social networks (Get Satisfaction - Incyte)

A survey of 1,200 consumers conducted by the CMO Council[3] measured motivations and expectations. They

---

[3] Consumers want better experience, deeper engagement, and more value from brands through social media; CMO - Chief Marketing Officer Council Worldwide, http://www.cmocouncil.org/press-detail.php?id=2819.

identified two reasons behind a "Like" placed on a page. Users do it to:

1. sign up to receive exclusive offers, discounts, and promotions;
2. share personal experiences and opinions regarding the brand with likeminded people.

As you see, becoming a "fan" does not mean being a fan in the commonly accepted sense of the term. A Facebook fan is not someone who roots for us, but someone who is expecting something from us. We have to give them a reason for being interested. And we must not try their patience, it just takes one click to be "unliked".

Image 24: A friend indeed.

Another study, conducted by 8thBridge[4] (see box below) also set out to clarify the reasons people put "Likes" on Facebook, and if they intend to share these recommendations with their friends. The results were extraordinary: social commerce appears not to work at all as is believed. The study reveals that people who click "Like" for one of our products are people who have already tried it and do indeed like it, rather than those who are potentially interested in purchasing it. Furthermore, the number of fans on a page was an influence in the purchasing decisions of not more than 35% of the interviewees.

---

[4] http://www.8thbridge.com/wpcontent/uploads/2011/09/Social_Commerce_IQ_Retail1.pdf.

Social Commerce IQ™: Retail
(8thbridge.com)

8thBridge conducted a survey and researched 200 retailers' fanpages on Facebook.

8thBridge surveyed 1,202 U.S. residents on their Facebook usage and interest in social commerce.

Survey questions included:

- Have you shared a product on Facebook?

- Have you asked for product recommendations on Facebook?

- Has a Facebook recommendation ever driven you to make a purchase?

- Do more Facebook Likes on a page increase the likelihood that you will buy that product?

- On a retailer's website that has the Facebook Like button, why would you click the Like button?

8thBridge's process to select the 200 retailers was as follows:

1. Select the 10 retailer categories from IR Top 500 Guide

2. Select the top 10-15 companies in each category based on the 2011 Internet Retailer overall

ranking.

3.   For each of these companies, 8thBridge selected retailers that have a significant presence on Facebook. [...]

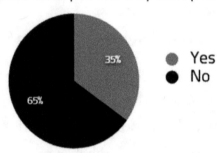

Do more Facebook Likes on a product page increase the likelihood that you will buy that product?

35%

65%

● Yes
● No

Image 25

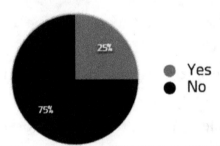

Have you shared a product on Facebook?

25%

75%

● Yes
● No

Image 26

Has a Facebook recommendation ever driven you to make a purchase?

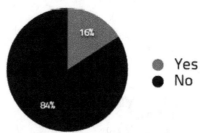

Yes
No

Image 27

Have you asked for product recommendations on Facebook?

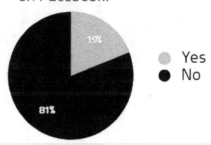

Yes
No

Image 28

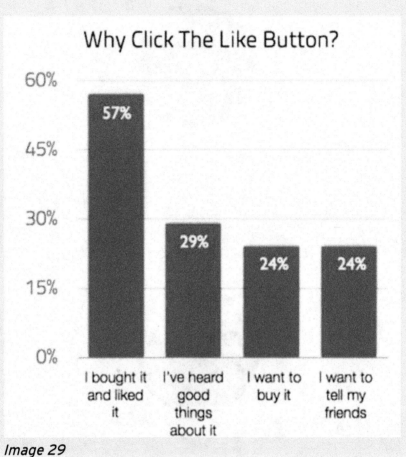

Image 29

http://www.8thbridge.com/wp-content/uploads/2011/09/Social_Commerce_IQ_Retail1.pdf

2.1.3. Fans: fanatic or apathetic?

How many fans are interested in interacting with companies or brands on Facebook? Hardly any.

A study of 400 million fans by Parker and Brian[5] reveals that updates are seen by only 3.5-7.49% of them. And even fewer do anything about it: a mere 0.25-0.90% respond to status updates.

Page Size (Fans)	Approximate % of Fans Seeing Posts Daily	Total Daily Impressions Per Fan	Unique Pageviews Per Fan
1,000 – 10,000	9.38%	0.6846	0.03191
10,001 – 100,000	6.02%	0.8347	0.06297
100,001 – 1,000,000	6.11%	0.5706	0.02333
1,000,000+	2.79%	0.5664	0.009506
OVERALL AVERAGE	7.49%	0.1401	0.001492

Image 30: With fans like these...

This means, for example, that out of 50,000 fans, there are only 450, at most, who are "good ones", who actually respond and show interest.

A metric that is often used to assess the level of engagement is "People talking about this". It is measured by Facebook Insights, which looks at the "stories" about us created by our fans.

---

[5] Parker e Brian, Shocker: 3% to 7,5% of fans see your page's posts, http://www.allfacebook.com/shocker-3-to-7-5-of-fans-see-your-pages-posts-2011-06.

A user creates a "story", for example, by:

- becoming a fan of a page
- putting "Like" on something (a post)
- commenting on or sharing a post
- responding to a question or invitation.

Another recent study[6] (Ehrenberg-Bass Institute: unfortunately the text of the study is not available, but it has been cited by Urs E. Gattiger on Commetrics.com) analysed the overall growth of fans for 200 brands on Facebook over a period of six weeks starting in October 2011. Their data shows that the overall percentage of fans who where "talking about this" was 1.3%. Excluding the new "Likes" and focusing on actions that imply more effective actual engagement, we are left with a measly 0.45%. According to this study, less than one half of one percent of the fans of a brand are interested in any sort of interaction with the brand.

Here is food for thought for when you hear talk of "user interaction". A few days ago it was discovered that Facebook totals the "Likes" automatically, without it necessarily corresponding to an actual "Like". If you have a "Like" counter on your site (a Facebook plug-in), don't

---

[6] Urs Gattiger, http://commetrics.com/articles/2012-2-trend-briefing-series-failure-to-communicate/.

delude yourselves that the number of "Likes" indicates anything real.

So what does that number represent? The authors of a study carried out in the United States[7] discovered that without clicking on "Like", but just by sending a link to a page in a private Facebook message, the counter goes up by one or two units. And it also goes up if you share a link on your page, or just comment on it.

Facebook defended itself only regarding the bug that made the counter go up by two at a time, but not about the rest. In the Facebook developers guide[8], it is explained in detail that the number of "Likes" gets counted on the basis of various actions, four to be precise, including the content of private messages. So in a certain sense, Facebook is spying on your private correspondence.

It was not long before the word "fraud" began to be used. Alan Woodward, professor at the University of Surrey, astutely commented: "Something intended for one purpose is being used for something completely different. What else is being done automatically that we don't know about?"

---

[7] http://www.bbc.co.uk/news/technology-19832043.

[8] https://developers.facebook.com/docs/reference/plugins/like/.

2.2. Does Advertising on Facebook Really Work?

2.2.1. My Kingdom for a Click

A way of measuring the effectiveness of an online advertising campaign is the Click-Through Rate (CTR). It represents the percentage of times that an ad has motivated a user to click on it. It has long been known (see the Webtrends[9] study of over 11,000 advertising campaigns) that the CTR for Facebook ads is low, about half that of web banners on non-Facebook pages.

Facebook Advertising Performance Benchmarks & Insights
By Webtrends

This report contains an analysis of over 11 thousand ads and is intended to provide a market reference for Facebook ad performance. It is worth noting that the majority of campaigns we analysed were focused on fan acquisition, which may skew some of the results.

---

[9] Webtrends: http://f.cl.ly/items/2m1y0K2A062x0e2k442l/facebook-advertising-performance.pdf.

Benchmarks may vary for campaigns aimed at websites or fan nurturing campaigns.

We focused on a few key metrics:
- Click-Through Rate (CTR)
- Cost per Click (CPC)
- Cost per Thousand (CPM)
- Cost per Fan (CPF)

Social Brands perform better

In a recent international survey fans stated that they are still primarily on Facebook for fun. Therefore it stands to reason that industries that are fun to discuss with our network are seeing higher CTR.

Facebook rewards social brands with cheaper prices

Brands that are social get a higher CTR, which translates into better engagement metrics: Post Quality Score, EdgeRank, Feedback Rate, and others. In turn, Facebook rewards such behaviour with a lower cost per click and greater visibility in the News Feed.

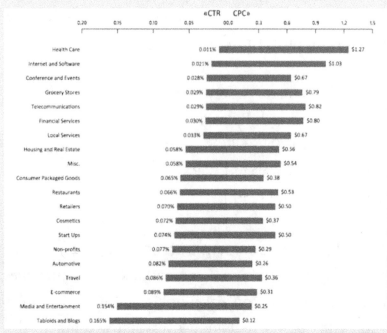

Image 31: How CTR and CPC vary according to categories

Social ads have a short shelf life

If you're used to buying search ads, you know that successful ads can be run for months without any changes. Out of the ads we measured, we found that interest targeted ads began to burn out after three to five days. Eventually the rotting CTR leads to Facebook deactivating the ad and it's back to the drawing board. Search ads don't have this problem because the ads are served to new people that search for the terms.

Social ads, however, target people which eventually leads to ad blindness.

The typical pattern is below.

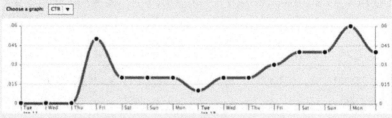

Image 32: CTR last for social ads

Friend-of-Fan targeting combats ad burnout

When using friend-of-fan targeting, marketeers can fight off the ad burnout problem. What happens is that as new fans are added, the circle for ad exposure increases, as does the amount of friend names below the ad. Eventually these ads burn out too, but they can last two to three times as long.

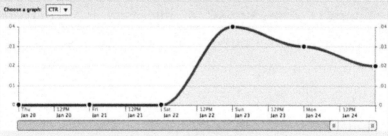

Image 33: CTR last for social ads- target: friend of fan

http://f.cl.ly/items/2m1yOK2AO62xOe2k442l/facebook-advertising-performance.pdf

Advertising on Facebook does not appear to be very effective. If we compare it to Google Adwords, its main competitor, it has less reach: 51% of all internet users, while Google reaches 90%. Facebook's CTR is 0.051%, Google's is 0.4%, and the overall average is 0.1%. Furthermore, Google offers a wider variety of publicity formats: text, images, videos, text on video, online video games that can also be played on mobile devices, etc.

Why does advertising perform so poorly on Facebook? We may find the answer in the very nature of the platform, and the different attitude of users with respect to those who are looking for something using Google (and who may end up finding it on a company website). Facebook is full of distractions, which is exactly why the users are there in the first place. Advertising on Facebook is irritating to users, and worse yet, it is awash in a sea of interesting things. And it makes no difference if the advertising campaign targets a specific set of interests, as we have seen clearly in the above study.

Google, on the other hand, with minimal graphics, captures users right when they are focused on a specific search and (discreetly) displays relevant ads. And the big plus of these ads is that they direct users to dedicated web pages that effectively convey the desired message or services, free of the data use policies of a social network owned by a third party.

2.2.2. An Army of Robots Clicking on Your Ads

If, in spite of everything, we still want to acquire advertising space on Facebook, we could decide to pay for it on a CPC basis, that is, we only pay if the ad actually gets clicked on. But can we be sure that those clicks are from human beings who are interested in what we are selling?

There was recently a big uproar about the case of the American start-up record label Limited Run. A few weeks ago, they wrote on their Facebook page[10] that they were going to delete their page and move away from Facebook. Here's what they said:

"A couple of months ago, when we were preparing to launch the new Limited Run, we started to experiment with Facebook ads. Unfortunately, while testing its ad system, we noticed some very strange things. Facebook was charging us for clicks, yet we could only verify about 20 percent of them actually showing up on our site. At first, we thought it was our analytics service. We tried signing up for a handful of other big-name companies, and still, we couldn't verify more than 15 percent to 20 percent of clicks.

"So we did what any good developers would do: We built our own analytic software. Here's what we found: On

[10] Limited Run: http://blog.limitedrun.com/post/28341629174/updated-weve-deleted-our-facebook-page.

about 80 percent of the clicks Facebook was charging us for, JavaScript wasn't on. And if the person clicking the ad doesn't have JavaScript, it's very difficult for an analytics service to verify the click. What's important here is that in all of our years of experience, only about 1 percent to 2 percent of people coming to us have JavaScript disabled, not 80 percent, like these clicks coming from Facebook.

"So we did what any good developers would do: We built a page logger. Any time a page was loaded, we'd keep track of it. You know what we found? The 80 percent of clicks we were paying for were from bots."

You read right, 80 percent of clicks. Let's assume Limited Run is telling the truth. Facebook makes 4 billion dollars a year in advertising alone. Eighty percent of 4 billion dollars is over 3 billion dollars: that means companies are giving Facebook 3 billion dollars without getting anything in return, all because of robotic clicks. And then of course there is all the money they spent beforehand on strategic consulting services to decide what sort of advertising investment to make!

Limited Run tried to contact Facebook to discuss its concerns, but they encountered only silence … until the news got around (and after the company had already decided to delete its fanpage). Another complaint lodged by the company regarded a name change:

"While we were testing Facebook ads, we were also trying to get Facebook to let us change our name, because we're not Limited Pressing anymore. We contacted them on many occasions about this. Finally, we got a call from someone at Facebook. They said they would allow us to change our name. [...] But only if we agreed to spend $2,000 or more in advertising per month – that's correct: Facebook was holding our name hostage. [...] This is why we need to delete this page and move away from Facebook."

Regardless of whether Facebook actually held their name hostage or deployed the bots that clicked on their ads, it is clear that we are using a platform that does not belong to us and we have to abide by the terms and conditions set forth by the owners of that platform (we will discuss this in greater depth in Chapter 3). But regarding fake clicks, a pertinent question might be: why doesn't Facebook take measures to stop them? Is it possible that no suspicions are raised even by profiles with such a high number of "Likes" per day or per month? This, instead, was Facebook's response:

"We have seen no signs of a significant problem, nor have we had reports from our advertisers, who are reaping positive results from their advertising campaigns on Facebook."

And yet Facebook is well aware of the problem. The issue had been raised as early as 2009. Advertisers had complained about the advertising that was costing them an arm and a leg. Facebook's click count did not correspond to the results obtained by using tracking software. The news was aired on the blog Wickedfire. However, the cause wasn't bots, but a bug that caused Facebook to count a higher number (more than 20% higher) of clicks than actually occurred. Some cried fraud. Facebook admitted the bug and eliminated it, but a shadow has remained.

If Facebook is still closing one eye, we could easily suspect that it is because bots mean more clicks and more clicks means more advertising revenue. Indeed, a few days after the great ruckus in the media raised by the case, Facebook finally revealed that 8.7% of its 955 million active users were duplicate or fake accounts. It stressed that these accounts are not welcome and that it will make an effort to eliminate them.

Indeed, starting on 27 September, it seems that something actually began to happen. The great purification has started, if reports are true that even major brands have witnessed significant losses in fans. According to the start-up Likester[11], which tracks the popularity of people and

---

[11] http://www.businessinsider.com/these-20-brands-lost-the-most-facebook-likes-the-day-of-the-fake-fan-purge-2012-10#5-coca-cola-lost-96445-likes-in-one-day-16.

pages on Facebook, Nokia lost 13,971 fans in one day, McDonald's 22,446 with Disney and Sony losing similar numbers, and Coca-Cola lost a whopping 96,445, again in one day.

But this is still a very serious problem. On the one hand, it is obvious that this whole story of the fake clicks and fake users undermines the credibility of the Facebook advertising system, threatening to bring it down like a castle of cards. On the other, if, as announced by Facebook Security, the cleanup of the fake accounts will affect less than 1% of the total "Likes" when 9% of the accounts are fake, the math just doesn't add up...

Image 34: Easy come, easy go

2.3. The Legend of Social Commerce

For some time now, the companies that naively thought of Facebook as a market … a bargain market … have had to reconsider this view. The plan of creating fanpages with millions of fans (and a considerable investment) and then transforming those fans into customers has turned out to be a pipe dream. In the United States, for example, major companies such as Gap, Nordstrom, GameStop and J.C. Penney all opened a shop on Facebook in 2011 and closed it before the end of the year.

Ashley Sheetz, vice president of marketing and strategy for GameStop, explained to *Bloomberg*[12]: "We just didn't get the return on investment we needed from the Facebook market, so we shut it down pretty quickly. For us, it's been a way we communicate with customers on deals, not a place to sell."

But why haven't the Facebook stores been successful? For the usual reasons. Facebook is a virtual meeting place, a place to go when you want to disengage, seek distraction, and have fun. It is not a supermarket, it is not a shopping centre.

---

[12] http://articles.businessinsider.com/2012-02-19/tech/31076370_1_zynga-facebook-market-e-commerce

The problem may lie with the structure of Facebook. Jeff Bercovivi (Forbes) points out how it differs from Pinterest. If being on Facebook is like being in a bar, being on Pinterest is like going to a trade fair. Most of these companies are losing money in their efforts to colonize Facebook because the development costs are too high.

Facebook, at the moment, is not built for that type of shopping experience. It should develop instruments like Pinterest to work. But to each his own: a shopping centre sells products, a bar entertains patrons...

2.4 ROI: Return of Illusions

Does it make sense to talk about ROI with social media? Before we start looking into this issue, we should remind ourselves exactly what ROI is.

ROI (Return on Investment) is a financial metric, a Key Performance Indicator (KPI) that comprises a formula for calculating the return on invested capital:

ROI= Net Profit / Invested Capital.

As pointed out by certain authors (Blanchard, Social Media ROI: Managing and Measuring Social Media Efforts in

Your Organization, Que Biz Tech), since ROI is a financial indicator, it must refer to a specific activity and be associated with a specific business objective. It does not make sense to ask, "What is the ROI for Facebook?" but rather "What ROI can one expect, in this period of time, from having a Facebook page?"

But even phrased in this way, the question is not easy to answer. How can you measure the profit from a Facebook page? Profit in this sense can only be measured if you can track things directly, for example, if you can verify that Facebook brought a customer to your platform. In the case of e-commerce, for example, if I receive a click on my website from a Facebook link and that click becomes a sale, I know that the money invested in the Facebook page has come back to me and I can make some calculations. Otherwise it doesn't make any sense to talk about ROI– by the very definition of the term.

And yet many do talk about it, even the so-called experts. But no one seems to be able to provide a convincing method for calculating it. The position of many authors is: "It doesn't make sense to talk about ROI for social media, but we talk about it anyway for the sake of convenience." What?? Talking about ROI just muddies things even further. And the truth is that it is used inappropriately. However ROI has become a synonym for "return on something", something in general, anything: money, oranges, fans, followers, or illusions, it doesn't matter. For example, if I invest x euros in Twitter and obtain n followers, I can calculate a nice ROI– but what I really want back are my euros! Don't trust agencies that talk glibly about ROI for social media: social networks are qualitative tools and it is very difficult to quantify a return.

Social media marketing is only a small part of digital marketing. If used without direct tracking of users, social networks can give you a positive ROI only in terms of qualitative parameters such as increase in brand awareness. If there is an ROI, it will be indirect and not quantifiable. If you try to assess the ROI of social media alone, isolated from an overall digital marketing strategy, you are probably barking up the wrong tree.

A recent study by Alessandro Vitale[13] is worth citing here. Based on data from Google Analytics, the study examined 8 websites. Two of them were especially significant, both with highly popular and active social profiles. One was running AdWords campaigns. Out of 44,000 visits, there were only 17 "effective conversions" from the social networks to an actual sale, whereas from AdWords, the rate is 60%. Things are even worse on the other site: 248,000 visits, 3,000 from social networks, only 148 traceable conversions.

---

[13]http://pro.dbatrade.com/wordpress/roi-social-network/.

This just provides further confirmation of the fact that potential is one thing, real figures are another. And we must not confuse the use of social networks for branding and using them to sell products.

2.5. Bots, Fake Comments, and Paid Reviews

2.5.1. You too are charmed by big numbers

Like all human beings, we are social animals. As social animals, we rate our success by how popular we are (and the males by the length of their iPhone). Social networks are structured in such a way that popularity is prominently featured in the most immediate way possible: a number. Whether it refers to views on YouTube, followers on Twitter or friends (fans) on Facebook, the number is the first thing that captures our attention, and it gives us a thrill.

In this regard, the number chase by companies might seem reasonable. It may be that companies (especially large ones) have determined that there is a critical mass of followers on Twitter that has to be reached before anyone will take them seriously, even though other studies[14] show that the number of fans of a brand only influences the purchasing decisions of 35% of users.

---

[14]http://www.8thbridge.com/wp-content/uploads/2011/09/Social_Commerce_IQ_Retail1.pdf.

Naturally, agencies have placed maximum emphasis on this parameter, reducing social media, whose conversational aspect they had much trumpeted, to a mere question of audience. And it is not difficult to imagine that many executives, lacking the cultural background for an effective assessment of the potential of the new media, let themselves get caught up in it.

Do more Facebook Likes on a product page increase the likelihood that you will buy that product?

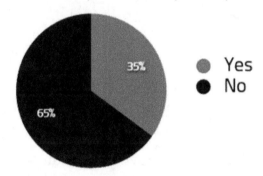

Image 35: 8thBridge study on social marketing (see box in Chapter 1)

The problem, as always, is not the numbers but the lack of strategy. What I am trying to demonstrate in this book is that it is pointless to have a gazillion fans on Facebook if you don't know what to do with them. It is useless to have thousands following us on Twitter if we have no idea where we're going! Again, success on social networks is a qualitative, not a quantitative, thing.

But these considerations aside, the essential point lies in the fact that **numbers are no longer a reliable indicator of success on social media**. The recent discoveries of bots and fake users, which I will talk about below, have blown the whole thing out of the water. Big numbers, especially if they surge suddenly, are more grounds for suspicion than admiration. Let's find out why.

2.5.2. Bots

People have been talking about bots for years, but only recently have they crept forth from the inner circles of specialists and spread out into the traditional media.

"Bot" is nothing more than an abbreviation for robot. It refers to a fake social network account that was not generated by a human being but by artificial means. The technical term for these pseudonymous identities is "sybil". These accounts are created automatically by a program that bypasses the request to resolve a CAPTCHA (Completely Automated Public Turing test to tell Computers and Humans Apart) at the time of registration. They may also be created manually, but it takes a long time to create any significant number of fake accounts. Then all it takes is a script to make great quantities of these accounts follow a chosen user. The phenomenon is known as "crowdturfing".

In addition to following a user, people with artificial profiles at their beck and call can be paid to leave fake comments, either positive or negative depending on the case. It is also a common practice among many administrators of Facebook pages to have a seedbed of alter egos that can be sowed as necessary to liven things up if they have become too quiet, nip controversies in the bud, or for a range of other purposes. As always, "everybody does it but no one is talking".

There are actually marketplaces that offer affiliation as an item of trade, where those who "sell" their profile– i.e., place it at the disposal of the buyer for a specific purpose– can acquire points that allow them to assemble a following worthy of note. It is a sort of Prostitution 2.0.

There are many digital agencies moving about in this murky scenario, managing social profiles for companies but not always in a manner that is entirely above board. They guarantee "effective" growth in fans and followers that may not effectively be real.

From the marketing standpoint, it may not be a bad strategy to acquire fake fans or followers. In some cases users may be favourably influenced by finding a fanpage with hordes of followers, and this could obviously be advantageous to the company. This is true especially in the start-up phase, populating the account to lure other customers in. It's a bit like when you choose to eat at the full restaurant rather than the empty one.

The real problem is when quantity is used by the web agencies to deceive their clients, the companies, regarding the real effectiveness of their work. I don't want to be a network cop rooting out the bad guys, but I would really like to see these deceptions stop because they cloud the perception of the real effectiveness of these tools, which then end up being like drugs: the big numbers give an initial rush that is just soooo great, man. But then the effect vanishes, reality hits, and you crash.

Facebook recently revealed that 8.7% of its 955 million active users are actually duplicate or fake accounts. This 8.7% consists of three categories: duplicate accounts, irregular accounts, and undesirable accounts.

Duplicate accounts represent 4.8% of total Facebook accounts. There are then 22.9 million irregular accounts (2.4%). The undesirable accounts, the dregs of Facebook, make up the remaining 1.5%. It may seem like a small number, but we are talking about 14.3 million profiles that violate the terms of service because they were created and are used to propagate spam. Facebook has also revealed that many of these undesirable accounts originate in developing countries.

Researchers at the University of California[15] examined these practices in China and found hucksters dealing in fake Facebook comments and reviews: *Likes* and followers for a few cents apiece.

Things are not much different on Twitter. For a few dollars you can buy hundreds or thousands of fake followers whose quality, i.e., how real they seem, depends on their price. I myself tried it out, getting 50,000 fake followers for the modicum price of 20 dollars. This does not violate Twitter's terms of service. But to make sure I got the whole package, I also bought 6,000 "Likes" for my Facebook page for 30 dollars.

Sudden surges in numbers of followers should always be viewed with suspicion. This happened recently to Mitt Romney, whose Twitter account grew by 20,000 and even 90,000 followers a day[16]. Lady Gaga is also purported to have 30,000 fake followers.

I do not mean to say that anyone with lots of followers or fans, or sudden growth spurts in their numbers, has

[15]   http://nastalenttalk.com/2012/08/22/likes-and-followersand-bots-why-mere-numbers-dont-tell-the-whole-social-media-story-2/

[16] 140 Elect: http://140elect.com/twitter-political-consulting-services/mitt-romney/.

purchased bots. The question is complex and delicate. It is true that it is easy to get them, there are many providers, but oftentimes the fakes attach themselves on their own, adhering in particular to well populated pages for spamming purposes. However, the implications are enormous. Think about stars with huge followings who are paid to promote a product to their audience, tens of thousands of people. What would happen if the advertiser found out that a good portion of those people were fake? And this is something that is happening more and more often.

2.5.3. A hunt for fakes

After my adventure purchasing fake followers, I decided to delve a little deeper and find out if I could develop a way to determine whether a user is real or fake. A sure-fire method does not exist. It is not possible to distinguish with absolute certainty a fake follower from a real one, unless of course you have direct knowledge of the specific case. Nevertheless, I tried to identify typical characteristics and elements of real users and bots in my study[17].

I created a program with an ad hoc algorithm that assigns points for "human" vs. "bot" behaviours to a sample of followers. The method and algorithm were developed according to criteria that I personally consider valid and

---

[17] See digitalevaluations.com.

sustainable, but other researchers might apply different values to the parameters or use different methods, thus obtaining different results.

The results were impressive, both the initial ones focusing on companies, and subsequent data acquired in reference to politicians. Many of the companies analysed had percentages of around 45% for fake followers. When I released my results regarding followers of Beppe Grillo, former Italian satirical comedian and now promoter of a new Italian political movement, they showed that over half of his approximately 600,000 fans may be sybils.

Table 1 Summary number of "Inactive or BOT" Projection on the Total:	
Account ID	Number of "Inactive or BOT"
BarackObama	5,326,883
MittRomney	178,237

Image 36

Table 1 Projection on the Total:							
Account ID	Followers	Number "Inactive/BOT"	%"inactive/BOT"	Number humans	%humans	%protected	%uncertain
BarackObama	17,820,968	5,326,883	29.89	8,020,826	45.01	11.56	13.54
MittRomney	814,734	178,237	21.88	405,357	49.75	13.64	14.73

Image 37: Obama's and Romney's bots

Table 1a Projection on the Total: International companies in the world							
Account ID	Followers	Number of bots	%bots	Number of Humans	%Humans	% Protected	%Uncertain
DellOutlet	1520302	699187	45.99	460499	30.29	10.52	13.20
WholeFoods	2565369	1137228	44.33	1103365	43.01	3.66	9.00
JetBlue	1674437	613514	36.64	667765	39.88	11.24	12.24
EA	927690	275524	29.70	490562	52.88	6.10	11.32
YSL	904271	222903	24.65	494817	54.72	8.37	12.26
SouthwestAir	1297848	300841	23.18	697723	53.76	12.10	10.96
threadless	1847061	350572	18.98	1095122	59.29	10.49	11.24
pepsi	755547	119905	15.87	458164	60.64	11.30	12.19
BlackBerry	977437	150037	15.35	604545	61.85	11.07	11.73
CocaCola	548512	72020	13.13	320605	58.45	11.94	16.48
PlayStation	1297768	150671	11.61	831869	64.10	12.99	11.30
SamsungMobile	1286753	136010	10.57	790967	61.04	14.98	12.98
Starbucks	2529115	174005	6.88	1695545	67.04	16.89	9.19

Image 38: Bot percentages in main international companies

The international press also picked up the study, and since then, a number of programs have been developed that analyse profiles for free to root out fake fans and followers. One of these is Fakers (the name suggesting that the real fakes are the ones who *have* lots of fake followers...) by Status People, which gained great popularity after publishing shocking results regarding President Obama's followers as well as those of celebrities such as Lady Gaga.

The problem with these tools is that the algorithm they are based on is not public, nor are the criteria used to distinguish between human and fake. How can you know if the numbers are realistic or not? In spite of their evident and well discussed weaknesses, these tools– or rather, what they show– have ignited outrage (the media, as usual, are having a field day with them) and may be changing, perhaps for the first time, the perception of a large segment of the audience with regard to social media and their booming numbers.

This is another reason why it is perfectly reasonable to believe that in the future users will increasingly seek out "trusted sources", i.e., company websites where the attraction is not big numbers but the reliability of information and user comments guaranteed by feedback mechanisms.

2.6. Prisoners of Facebook

Generally, when you are at someone else's house you are on your best behaviour, trying at least not to be a nuisance for your host. The same thing is true if we use a social platform that doesn't belong to us.

Facebook dictates the terms and conditions and we have to accept them. I am not seeking to polemicize, but this is something to think about, especially if you intend to concentrate your digital activity exclusively on this platform or others like it, letting the company website slowly decay. Part of the reason is that the above terms and conditions could change, and we can do nothing about it.

If you create a fanpage, you have to abide by certain rules. The problem is that sometimes the rules are not clear and may in any case be open to interpretation. The really big problem is that a violation of these rules could lead to the immediate deletion of the page and the loss of all our precious fans, both human and robot– and there may be no way to get them back.

Image 39: By-laws and blue laws

The New Yorker was recently embroiled in just such a case[18]. The venerable U.S. magazine found itself banned from Facebook for a perfectly innocent cartoon showing Adam and Eve– in Edenic garb.

---

[18] http://www.newyorker.com/online/blogs/cartoonists/stevens-cartoon.

"Well, it was original."

Image 40: The cartoon that got the New Yorker banned from Facebook

The reason? Violation of rules regarding nudity and pornography, specifically the prohibition against the representation of "nipple bulges". Reports on our content by other users are taken into consideration by administrators. If someone reports us repeatedly for spam or violation of terms of use, we risk being banned.

The same fate suffered by the New Yorker also occurred with the fanpage of the A.C. Milan football club[19] in December 2010: reported for inappropriate content, it was

[19] Facebook chiude la pagina del Milan: http://www.gazzetta.it/Calcio/SerieA/Milan/13-11-2010/facebook-chiude-pagina-milan-711804537987.shtml.

closed down, leaving its million fans in the lurch. It turned out it was an ugly prank perpetrated by fans of rival teams at A.C. Milan's expense.

This episode reveals the extent to which Facebook is vulnerable to underhanded actions by competitors. We can easily imagine hearing in the future of cases where a page is deliberately seeded with fake fans that can then be reported to the media in order to discredit the user or company. No password is needed to purchase fake fans from third parties.

And as I have said repeatedly, the terms and conditions are not written in stone, they may change suddenly and unexpectedly at any time. Other items subject to such change are the graphics, user data policies, and Application Programming Interfaces (API) . Twitter, for example, recently limited functionalities that many companies had used to create entire management systems.

And as I am writing this, I have a problem with my blog: it is no longer possible for me to comment via Facebook because an update is not yet available for Wordpress, the platform for my blog.

We cannot know what changes to expect in the future. But just think what would happen if tomorrow Facebook decided that we can only access certain information about our friends by paying!

Limiting dialogue to the fanpage is a risk for companies, especially regarding the information about our fans, such as email addresses. It's like meeting a bunch of interesting people at a party, finding that many like you and are eager to talk to you, and then suddenly being kicked out of the house onto the street. How can you find the people you were just talking to if you don't have their telephone numbers? And how will they find you if you don't have a website?

Lady Gaga is considered the queen of Facebook and Twitter for her influence and number of followers. She recently created a vertical social network dedicated to her fans and followers, Littlemonsters.com. Her manager, Troy Carter explained the move: "There may come a day when you don't have the cover of *Vanity Fair*, or you may not be able to get on that big TV show. But it's important that you have that direct communication with that audience so they still know what you're doing." We will look at this in further detail in Chapter 3.

2.7. The Death of Facebook

Facebook now permeates our behaviours, habits, and conversations to the point where it is difficult to remember life before it. And yet we have some difficulty imagining that Facebook will exist forever in the way we now know it. On the one hand we all feel that it is not a trend, a passing fad like Second Life, for example. On the other we cannot help asking ourselves: if it ends, how will it end?

Sure, even the concept of "end" is relative. End does not mean disappearance: vinyl LPs have "ended", and yet they have not disappeared, just been pushed back into a niche.

Can we foresee the future of Facebook? The answer is no. There are no crystal balls, not even in the digital world. Nevertheless, we can examine the patient's medical history and try to come up with a prognosis.

Facebook isn't growing like it used to. In April 2012 it was growing by only 5% as compared to 24% one year earlier and 89% in April 2010. As Facebook levels off, Google+ and vertical networks, especially Pinterest and Instagram (the latter acquired by Facebook), are burgeoning. One of the most hotly debated current issues is the presumed "struggle for survival" between Facebook and

Google+. It's not clear why, but the question is put in terms of "only one will be left standing", perhaps inspired by the movie *Highlander*.

Google+ grew at a dizzying pace in its first year and is apparently the social network most similar to Facebook. Some see it as being superior because it indexes posts on Google search. However, I do not think that this is the real question. As I see it, Facebook does not need to be worried about competition from Google+, which is a horizontal network, it needs to be concerned about vertical networks. Let me explain the difference between the two.

Vertical social networks are those that address a niche. The niches may be defined in different ways and have various characteristics. So you may have people united by specific interests or purposes (Meetic for dates, MiGente for people with Latin-American origins, etc.). Niches may also be defined by content (Pinterest, just images and videos) or technology (Instagram, just content sharing from mobile devices). If Facebook is the neighbourhood bar, LinkedIn is the employment office. Sure, sooner or later we all either seek or offer employment, and indeed LinkedIn is highly populated, but it is still a niche network– or if you prefer, a theme network. Griddixcat is a social network for cat lovers. Couchsurfing is for travellers who want to find people who can put them up for a night. Instagram, the epitome of the vertical social network, is only for smartphone owners who want to share, via their smartphones, photos taken with vintage-effect filters built into their smartphones. There is no limit to community verticalization. And this is what Facebook should fear.

The more a social network is able to offer something specific that satisfies the needs of a user, the larger the piece of turf that it captures from Facebook. One thing is clear, if everyone is on Facebook, then there will also be people looking for dates, people of Latin-American origin, people seeking or offering employment, people who love cats, people looking for a couch to sleep on, and people who want to share faux-vintage photos. But it's so hard to find them, lost in such a huge crowd. It's like trying to navigate a crowded, noisy bar during happy hour. Lots of interesting people are there to relax and enjoy themselves, and while they are there they talk about this and that, whatever pops into their heads. But if they want to buy a car, they leave the bar and go to the dealer.

We do not have a lot of free time, and we will probably have even less in the future. And so we prefer to go where we can do exactly what we have set out to do in the most efficient way possible, instead of wasting time at the bar, i.e., on Facebook. Our tastes and needs will become progressively better refined and well defined– more verticalized– and we will become increasingly selective, seeking specific flavours, and more and more irritated by the din of a mixed crowd.

As for the adventure on the stock exchange, it is clear that so far it has been a flop. The IPO was too high, stocks selling for a fortune (38 dollars!), and a few months later, the insiders themselves selling off stock packages, like Zuckerberg, who sold 30 million (according to Hardcop).

And people begin to get tired of advertisements. Companies are not happy either. Facebook's own statistics state that an average of only 15% of fans see updates on the fanpage, perhaps because of the algorithm that regulates the newsfeed, or because of the distraction of the overwhelming quantity of inputs that are posted on Facebook every day. Word is out that they are experimenting with a "promoted status", where our updates are shown to our friends[20]. Thus for the price of 7 dollars per status, we can poke our friends in their home feed to get their attention. So even friendship is up for sale. Facebook is becoming increasingly commercial. Fair play, if it ever did exist, has been gone for some time now.

---

[20]http://www.repubblica.it/tecnologia/2012/10/04/news/facebook_l_amicizia_ora_si _compra-43842408/?ref=HRERO-2.

FACEBOOK: I WANT MY FRIENDS BACK!
The Dangerous Minds case: Facebook steals our friends and fans

An excellent post by **Dangerous Minds**[21] brings home the point about paid posts and what they really mean for a fanpage.

Starting in the spring of 2012, many began to notice that **their Facebook reach was diminishing**. It seemed that their posts no longer reached their entire fan base, but only a fraction of them. This was true not only for fanpages but also for individual users, who began to notice that they weren't getting regular updates in their newsfeeds from the pages they "liked", and they were also getting fewer updates from their friends.

Dangerous Minds discussed their own case on their blog. Since the spring of 2012, the growth in their fans (29,000 to 53,000) did not bring a corresponding increase in traffic to their blog from Facebook. Worse than that, this traffic actually *decreased* dramatically, by one half to two thirds. It's a bit like or-

---

[21]http://dangerousminds.net/comments/facebook_i_want_my_friends_back

ganizing a large rally and then discovering the microphone is broken and no one can hear you beyond the second row. And this is all happening in plain view.

Gokul Rajaram, Facebook advertising head, explained that a post reaches, on average, 15% of fans and that if you want to be sure of reaching the remaining 85%, "sponsoring posts is important". That's a gentle way to put it. What he means is: If you want to reach your fans– the ones you have spent great time and effort cultivating, the ones you used to reach free of charge– now you have to pay us.

But doesn't Facebook continue to repeat, on its access page, that it is **"free and always will be"**? To us it seems like the rules are being changed in the middle of the game, and it could be a suicidal move for Facebook. Why? Well, one thing is that it is a way of admitting that the platform is not performing well and needs a little push. Secondly because the prices imposed by Facebook for reaching 100% of your fans are prohibitive for many small and medium businesses.

For example, this is how they work out for Dangerous Minds:

53,000 fans
10 posts per day
$200 per post to reach 100% of fans
$2,000 per day
$14,000 per week
$56,000 per month
For a total of **$672,000** per year to get what used to be **completely free.**

Actually, Dangerous Minds publish from 10 to 16 posts per day, so this is a **conservative estimate.**

As Dangerous Minds point out, many brush this off with glib comments such as "this is just Capitalism, baby" and that if they don't like it users can simply slip off to free venues like Twitter or Google+. They fail to grasp the enormity of the thing. As Dangerous Minds write, this is the *"single most misguided thing a major corporation has ever deliberately done, bar none, in the entire history of American capitalism and the world."* It is an extremely dishonest and aggressive move that will only damage its users, who are, in the final analysis, its only strength.

Many small or medium enterprises that cannot deploy such a large advertising budget will be forced to abandon their fanpages. If a site lives off advertising and sells advertising space on the basis of the number of views it receives, but it has to pay Facebook more for the right to get these views than it gets from the resulting advertising revenue, what other choice does it have?

After having invested time and effort to assemble a fan base, I discover that 85% of my fans– people who have chosen to become fans and are anxious to receive news and updates from me– will no longer receive my posts unless I shell out an enormous amount of money. If I can't afford it, not only have I wasted my initial investment, but the fans who suddenly feel "ignored" might be offended, damaging not only my pocketbook but also my reputation.

Facebook has made a big mistake. It has upset everyone and projected an image of unbridled greed. It might have been enough to put a more reasonable price on sponsored posts. If many begin to emigrate, it will have struck a blow to its very essence. Picture a Facebook where the only updates you get in your newsfeed come from Coca Cola, Nike, and other large corporations that can afford the price. Who is going to want to spend any more time on Facebook?

It would certainly not be the first time that something "unsinkable" takes a plunge. And I am not referring to the Titanic, but to the battleship MySpace. Still appearing to be the world's pre-eminent social network in early 2008, it failed to perceive how user needs were changing, it did not know how to compete with Facebook and Twitter, and by last December it had become a desert.

Chapter 3
Adapt or Die: a new strategy

3.1. The Back Home Strategy

3.1.1. Ye were not made to live like unto brutes

… but for pursuit of virtue and knowledge. (Dante)

So far, we have focused on the limits of Facebook as a digital marketing tool. We have seen how Facebook is an excellent tool for listening to users, CRM, and branding, but it is often ineffective for engagement, data mapping, advertising, and e-commerce.

But I want to emphasize that Facebook is important. I would never advise a company to delete its Facebook page or not to open one in the first place. Quite the contrary! Facebook provides companies with an extraordinary opportunity to implement a complex and effective strategy: the Back Home Strategy. Let's see what it is.

The central theme of this chapter (and this book) is being informed. I would like companies and those leading them to understand exactly how to get the most out of digital tools, both those that are available to them free of charge and those that they create themselves. But misunderstandings arise every time I talk about the Back Home Strategy. I have been accused of being anti-Facebook. Nothing could be farther from the truth. I have nothing against social networks. And more to the point, I have no negative feelings about Facebook as a tool for digital marketing. The key here is that it has to be a tool, a means, and not an end in itself. It has to be used in an intelligent, informed, and discerning way within the context of a broader overall strategy.

Image 41: Unlocking the secrets to hospitality

Facebook may be seen as an ocean teeming with fish of all species. There are small and rather drab fish and then there are the splendid tropical species: these are my potential customers, and I want them for my aquarium. Well, this metaphor really doesn't work for me. I don't want to imprison the fish, and when I think of it, I have never really liked aquariums. So let's say that if Facebook is the ocean, my Home is the coral reef where Nemo lives. A safe, secure, and beautiful place where people like to come and visit, and where they like to bring their friends.

3.1.2. Digital survival strategies

At first glance, the digital world seems to be the realm of immediacy, of the short-lived, of fleeting contacts. And yet what many do not understand is that investing in digital media can bring long-term benefits, like building a solid house of bricks.

This shouldn't seem so strange if we really stop and think about it. Everything that we do online has something of the permanent. Everything leaves a trace. If history is being written online then the future may– no, must– also be planned online. It is a certainty: the more you invest in a long-term strategy, the more you get from it. The process is necessarily slow. It takes time to create a community, to give it appeal, to get people to join. Perhaps more time than it would take to gather a few thousand fans on Facebook. But there is a big difference in the end result. If you had to choose between having 10,000 fans (assuming they are all real) about whom you know nothing, apart from their names (again, assuming they are not just nicknames), and having 2,000 people in your *own* community, where you know their first and last names, ages, geographical zone, email, mobile phone, occupation, hobbies... which would you prefer?

The importance of information has long been recognized by people in the marketing business. If you know something about the people you are communicating with you also know how to approach them, and most importantly, you know if you can approach them. The more you know about your audience, the more you know what to say, how to say it, and when to say it. It's like the difference between shouting to a mixed crowd of distracted people (as we have seen, putting "Like" on a page is not a sign of interest) and having a conversation with a select group of people who find you interesting and are in the right mood. Facebook does allow you to do that, but you have to pay for the privilege (sponsored posts): an option that will become increasingly less effective and more expensive. It's the difference between traditional, generalist advertising, and targeted marketing.

So what role does Facebook play in all of this? Facebook is extremely important: it is the entry to my home, to my community. It is one of my major reservoirs of potential customers. It is the public square where they return, after a satisfying visit to my place, to spread the word. But that's not all. If someone enrols in my community via Facebook, I can ask them for permission to publish material on their timeline, perhaps triggering a viral process. If a person does an action of some sort at my place, I can let her friends know about it (although if I've really done things well, it will be she who spontaneously invites her friends to come and check it out!).

Investing in a long-term digital strategy means creating an architecture that reflects your own digital identity, building a solid environment comprising a central nucleus and many outreaching branches. However, there are still very few who have understood this or, having understood it, have the means to put it into practice. With the current economic crisis and its budget restrictions and reduced windows of opportunity, many marketeers prefer to seek short-term results. Minimum expense for maximum return. And social networks look just perfect for vindicating the strategy of "I want it all and I want it now"... especially if the yardstick for maximum return is number of followers. But as we've seen, it just doesn't measure up.

In this chapter I will give you an overview of the tools available and the sorts of results you can hope to achieve. You don't really have freedom of choice if you don't know what you have to choose from.

Key Social Business Strategies
1) Harnessing External Ecosystems
2) Relationship + Data Ownership & Control

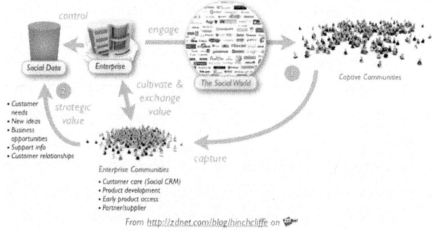

Image 42: Back Home Strategy diagram

3.1.3. What is the Back Home Strategy?

Back home, back to my company's home. But who is it that comes back? Users. OK, and where do they come from? From social networks. Social networks play a strategic role in the Back Home Strategy, there is no question about it. As you read on it will become increasingly hard to claim that I am preaching an anti-social-network gospel...

But apart from its metaphorical value, what exactly do we mean by *home*? My digital home is my base camp. It is a place that represents me clearly and officially. It comprises my company website, associated blogs and forums, extensions of the website dedicated to special projects, e-commerce stores, and my communities and vertical social networks. Here are the conclusions of the study by Get Satisfaction and the Incyte Group titled *To Monetize Open Social Networks, Invite Customers to Be More Than Just "Friends"*:

Because consumers spend so much time engaging in open social networks like Facebook and Twitter, marketeers can strategically leverage them to build relationships with massive numbers of consumers. The problem is that "likes" aren't equivalent to "relationships" with customers. Clearly, there is a missing tool in the social marketeer's toolkit. They need to find a way to connect with consumers and address their explicit needs and desires more directly.

This study sheds new light on the missing tool that marketeers need to build strong relationships with consumers: a branded customer community. Without a customer community that the "brand" owns and proactively manages, social media strategies are simply incomplete. Think of Facebook, Pinterest, and Twitter as doors, and until you invite your 'friends' into your branded customer community where they can 'talk' with each other and with you directly about your products and services, you're essentially leaving them out in the cold. The community can have an entry point on your Facebook brand page, but your consumers want to interact with you in your branded customer community, not their open social networks.

from the conclusions of the Get Satisfaction - Incyte Group paper: To Monetize Open Social Networks, Invite Customers to Be More Than Just "Friends".

You are already wondering: "Do I really need the Back Home Strategy and all this other stuff?" It's a perfectly legitimate question, but it doesn't have a single straightforward answer. What you need exactly and what you can confidently do without depends on who you are and what you are aiming to achieve. This is what you need to decide when you map out your strategy.

It might seem excessive, for example, to create your own social platform. And perhaps it is. But remember, people who come to my home have to find a welcoming and enriching experience that will inspire them to bring their friends. And a social platform is an excellent way to generate this engagement.

Today's web users are demanding and they know the ropes. They are accustomed to the usability of social networks and to the incredible possibilities they offer for sharing and accessing content. You can't give them a sop, they will never be interested in a website filled with colourful animations that delight the CEO but will never attract any fellow viewers. You need advanced functionalities, and these require an excellent development team and a great deal of personalization. If you want to be credible you have to do things right, entrusting the work to accomplished professionals. The only ones who are successful in the digital world today are those who invest the necessary resources: the myth of everything for free is precisely a myth and inexorably leads companies off track.

You have to get into the mind-set of investing what you have to invest. And it may be a lot. It's true that there are pre-packaged open-source programs you can use (Wordpress, Joomla, etc.), but there is no guarantee that will meet your needs perfectly. Depending on the functionalities you want, you have to know whether to go to the tailor or to the retail outlet, whether to start from zero or cobble something together from pieces that already exist.

One thing is sure: Home represents MY place, and it stands whether Facebook (or whatever social network rises to take its place) is there or not. It is a central engine with the appropriate complement of extensions: mobile applications and Facebook apps. These tools are an integral part of the Back Home Strategy. Let's take a look at them.

3.1.4. Back Home Strategy tools

Mobile applications
Nowadays the app is an indispensable part of the digital experience that I, as an enlightened company, want to offer to my users. Looking to the future, it is easy to imagine that we will be increasingly and more constantly interconnected. It is important that your website is optimized for

every device, but also that every device is exploited to its fullest capacity. The app makes this possible.

If we think about a smartphone and everything we can do with it, we can come up with ideas of what we can offer with an app. Photos, videos, QR codes, immediate file sharing... Thanks to smartphones and tablets, the individual's day-to-day experience immediately feeds into the social dimension of the network. This development is far too important and pervasive to be ignored.

Here too it is well worth seeking out the services of competent professionals to avoid costly mistakes. A mobile application has to be conceived and designed to work on all types of mobile device. At the moment there are at least four: iOS, Android, Windows Phone, and Blackberry, with various versions of firmware and screens of different sizes.

A serious app has to work with all operating systems and run on all the associated devices. There is nothing more irritating to a user than feeling he is being discriminated against: why have they only released an app for the iPhone?! But producing an app for all platforms is costly. However, the difference between doing it or not doing it is pretty much the same as the difference between success and failure. And this consideration must also be extended to tablets, another quickly expanding market.

Facebook Apps

Although it may seem to be a contradiction in terms, in activating the bring-'em-back-home stratcgy, it is not at all necessary to oblige your users to exit Facebook and enter another site. It is actually possible to map user profiles without leaving the Facebook platform. There are Facebook apps precisely for this purpose.

But we must immediately make a distinction. The apps developed for Facebook– beyond the standard ones offered by the platform– come in two basic varieties. One is relatively simple and functions within Iframe. It is found between the left and right bars, under the header. It is a sort of "hole" with a link that points to an external address, for example, to my site. However, the content you see in that frame comes from *my* server, it is the equivalent of my site, my Home.

The other one, in FBML (Facebook Markup Language) is more complicated to program. It runs on Facebook, but here too, if it has to register data, it does so in my database.

So, as we see, planning an app for Facebook is by no means a contradiction. It should be clear that it is not a question of "bringing people to my site" at all costs. What we are interested in is knowing them. We want to know who they are and various things about them. We want to be able to save their information and map them. If they don't want to leave Facebook, it's not our problem. We can create our site (Home) on Facebook with our own database. We don't care about bringing people to our site, we want to bring them to our home!

3.1.5. Choose your users

Lady Gaga has more than 53 million fans. How did she do it? Easy, by being Lady Gaga. But not all of us are Lady Gaga– unluckily or luckily, depending on your point of view. If, for example, my company produces butter, I've just got to face the facts: even if my produce is the creami-est, tastiest, and healthiest butter ever, one that has been on the market since 1912 and even helps people slim down and lower their cholesterol, it will never have a fan base as huge and spontaneous as Lady Gaga's. My butter will never be Lady Gaga. We're going to have to resign ourselves to the fact that the ways of the market are infin-itely unfair.

Users come in two flavours. We have what we might call "organic" traffic: people who arrive spontaneously and are generally already fans. So much the better! But I want my bread buttered on both sides (the metaphor seems appro-priate here). So I also want to go after a second group of users. And I am going to have to work a bit to get them. I have to invest time, money, and energy. Do I want to take this whole investment, together with all my great hopes, and pitch it into the churning chaos of Facebook? Or do I want some guarantee that I will be getting something back from it?

If I have acquired– and deserve– someone's attention, interest and sympathies, I want that person to come and visit me where I "live". I want her to join my community and I want to know a few things about her: with her permission, of course. I have organized a party and want to invite her. She may bring something to drink, but since I've never really cared for champagne, I'd rather have her information.

3.1.6. Why people should come to me

This is the critical point of the whole strategy. The centre of gravity that moves people and attracts them to me from the social networks is my *Home*.

My creative team has to get to work to find some good reasons for people to move away momentarily from the basic Facebook tools and come pay me a visit. And this is true regardless of whether or not an effective Back Home Strategy has been implemented. If you don't have any good ideas for them they are not going to talk about your butter even on Facebook.

WHAT TO DO ON FACEBOOK...	...HOW TO CONTINUE BACK HOME
Share links...	killer content
e-Commerce offers...	e-Store
Contest announcement...	information, registration, announcement of winners
Ads for special offers...	download coupon
Automatic post on timeline...	vote, upload material, other actions

Image 43: Integration between Facebook and Home

Considering people's attachment to Facebook, my creative team will obviously have to be talented. If they are really talented, visitors will come back to me another time. And if they are super talented, people will not only come and then return, but they will join my branded community and invite their friends to come along. My customer will end up working for me.

The goal of the creative team, of the content they develop, is to give meaning to my community. If what I produce is butter, people will never line up spontaneously to become a part of my community. But if I offer innovative, intriguing content and useful or rewarding functionalities, this might change.

Let us suppose (but please don't restrict yourselves to this humble example) that I, butter producer (just to take an extreme case), organize "buttery events" around the world, exclusive parties where the menu consists of buttery hors-d'oeuvres, where you can win a lifetime's supply of butter, and where this year's Miss Butter is elected, complete with calendar. And let's suppose I release useful mobile phone apps, a selection of delicious recipes using butter, information about special deals, etc. People would begin to find reasons to come and check me out.

But that's not all. I could become the benchmark for butter and butter-related activities, so high powered that I become the champion in my area and my competitors all come to play on my field. Indeed, some companies have adopted this approach, making their competitors become part of the content.

There are many ways to offer interesting content. But I should explain exactly what I mean by "interesting".

Something that is interesting for a user is something that gives an immediate benefit (promotions, discounts) or a prospective one (prize contests, giveaways, etc.). Something is interesting if, like social networks, it exploits the "Warhol effect" : the promise of being famous for fifteen minutes. This might be represented by authoring an article on the company blog (or even opening your own space), a photography contest, a contest of the type "personalize product X and have people vote for it on Facebook", or "upload your video or song", or even the usual humdrum beauty contest.

Economic benefits or visibility, whose purpose is to attract users, are then complemented with killer content: not just a few bits of information on the company and its history (which has to be there in any case), but something more eye-opening, something that might start a buzz, or even a debate if necessary. Something that people want to share right away on their timeline. Here you need to do a good job of content preparation, regardless of whether things take place at my home or on Facebook. In general, company archives hold a treasure trove of interesting material: information sheets, images of historical products, historical documents, material from old publicity campaigns... The content has to be very specific, vertical. Imagine we are butter producers and that every day we go searching for news, curiosities, recipes, controversies, and other items involving butter. These might be old advertisements, displays, projects you have sponsored. We should use a light tone, one befitting a "butter magazine". You can– no, you must– go as deeply into the specifics as you like. You're in your own home here. And furthermore, you will have more material to share on Facebook.

Below we present a number of interesting discoveries regarding the Home (branded sites) and what it is that attracts users.

Branded communities and customer needs

from: To Monetize Open Social Networks, Invite Customers to Be More Than Just "Friends" (Get Satisfaction - Incyte Group)

Relevant content is what drives consumers to prefer branded communities.

Incyte asked consumers what customer community activities they would most likely participate in:
- Read content – 32.5%
- Share Content – 19.5%
- Learn from others – 18.1%

Consumers are clearly saying that a primary value proposition of a customer community is that it allows them to quickly access information that is relevant and accurate – and they prefer it when that information is provided by other people like them.

What attracts them to customer communities is the relevancy of the content to their needs presale, at the point of sale, and post-sale.

When asked which of the following activities they would most likely participate in on these sites, results showed the following trends:

- Read content – 27.3%
- Follow posts – 18.8%
- Share with social network – 18.2%
- "Liking" – 8.9%
- Posting replies and answers – 8.3%
- Chatting – 5.9%

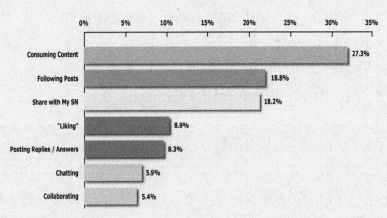

Image 44: what attracts consumers to branded customer communities

Note that the vast majority of time on branded customer community sites is spent consuming content and following posts. Why? Because content – both company and consumer created – is king.

http://info.getsatisfaction.com/rs/getsatisfaction/images/In-cyteGroup_Whitepaper_Q32012.pdf

3.1.7. Who's who of the Back Home Strategy

CASE 1: OBAMA-BIDEN

Like Lady Gaga, Barack Obama owes much of his success to the intelligent and strategic use of social networks. According to Arianna Huffington, "Were it not for the internet, Obama would not be President." His victory in 2008 has been nicknamed "the Facebook Election".

Obama has continued to develop his digital campaign with great care during the current election year as well: he has a presence on Instagram, on Reddit with AMA-Ask Me Anything, on Twitter, LinkedIn and Facebook, Foursquare and Google+. His wife Michelle is also very active on the major social networks.

And again like Lady Gaga, Obama also felt the need to establish his own online space. Back in 2008, the President's digital staff created My.BarackObama.com. This year the site has evolved further and become Dashboard. Dashboard is a platform where the President's supporters can gather to organize the re-election campaign, promote events, propose new initiatives, and keep up to date at all times.

As well as the social aspects, Dashboard also leverages competitiveness. The hope is to stir up the ambitions of local groups and spur them to be the best at achieving objectives, such as the greatest number of phone calls made, doors knocked on, or new voters registered.

Naturally, the tool allows the President's staff to collect a great deal of information about his constituents. When users register they are only asked to provide their email, mailing address and zip code. But then they are taken to another login page that can also be reached via Facebook, thus allowing access to additional user information, such as the basic information about their friends. This wealth of information remains available to the presidential team to pursue the electoral marketing campaign through other channels.

CASE 2: TICKETMASTER

Ticketmaster, world leader in online ticket sales, conducted a study where it found that every time someone purchased a ticket online, they shared the position of their seat with their friends on Facebook. Bringing this social aspect to online ticket purchasing means more money can be earned by the company (estimated at 5 dollars per purchase). Hence the Facebook app was developed to allow online ticket purchasers to show their seat position to their friends, who would then be motivated to purchase nearby seats.

Of course, the app depends on the user giving permission to access basic information (name, profile picture, sex, list of friends, etc.) and other items from the user profile (likes, etc.). The application is a bona fide online ticket office, where users can seek events and purchase tickets, but it also integrates social aspects such as the possibility to let friends know what events you have chosen and invite them to come along. Hence, without leaving Facebook, Ticketmaster has found a way to exploit the potentialities of the network while also gaining more information about its own users.

Kip Levin of Ticketmaster comments: "This is the first time ever we actually allow somebody to stay inside Facebook to complete the purchase; they don't have to link back to the Ticketmaster website." The integration with Spotify is another plus. Once permission has been granted, the app looks at listener data and uses it to recommend shows and events. "So instead of them coming to the web page where we're just saying 'here are the top-selling shows', we can show them a list of shows based on what they're listening to."

Various Ticketmaster competitors have used Facebook's Open Graph to sell tickets, but none of them provide interactive seating maps or suggestions based on musical tastes and do so in close to real time.

So here is an example of the Back Home Strategy based on optimal integration between the Home and Facebook. In this case, without even obliging users to leave Facebook, I can access their information and use it, among other things, to offer them an enhanced service. And considering that the Ticketmaster app records 480,000 users a month, we are talking about a very substantial amount of useful information netted by the company.

CASE 3: LADY GAGA

Lady Gaga is considered not only the queen of pop, but also the queen of social networks. Few can match her numbers. In 2010 she was the first artist to achieve a billion views on YouTube. She currently has some 30 million followers on Twitter (President Obama has 20 million), while her Facebook following exceeds 50 million.

The singer and her staff have grasped the importance of integrating social and traditional media. They know how to connect with their audience in real time and create effective content that is widely shared, resulting in a very high level of engagement.

For example, in the run-up to the launch of her disk *Born This Way* in May 2011, she set up partnerships with Zynga for GagaVille (a Gagaesque Farmville), VEVO for exclusive premieres, iTunes for the promotional countdown, Best Buy and Streaming to provide a signed copy of the disk, and Gilt Groupe and Amazon Cloud Player for special offers.

Given her success on consolidated social networks, Lady Gaga's decision to establish her own social network, Littlemonsters.com, raised quite a few eyebrows.

I see absolutely nothing illogical about her choice. Gaga and her staff must have realized that filling Facebook with valuable content reaching millions of people was more a favour to Facebook than to themselves. The Littlemonsters platform allows them to "own" this value. It was simple to see, partly because her fans were already spending time and energy on social networks dedicated to Germanotta such as Gaga Daily, Gaga News, and Lady-Gaga.net. Why not give them what they were clearly hankering for?

But make no mistake: Lady Gaga's social network does not stand in opposition to Facebook or Twitter and is not an alternative to them. It is perfectly integrated with both. Matt Michelsen, the CEO of Backplane, the start-up that created the network, explained that the purpose of Littlemonsters is to integrate with other social networks and to create a community, or as they say now, to verticalize. On Facebook all you can see is whether someone is a fan of Lady Gaga; on Littlemonsters, you see just how much of a fan they are, what concerts they have been to, etc.

Lady Gaga is known for her special effects and extravagant costumes: she is an eminently visible "brand". And so her social network stakes everything on image.

Its graphics are reminiscent of Pinterest (a board with photos), but it also has characteristics borrowed from other social media, such as Reddit's possibility to vote on content. In addition to the ability to publish or share images, each user profile page includes messages, events, news, and exclusive content. Members can "Like" other people's posts, share these likes on other social networks, comment on other people's content and help it go viral. Here the fan is king: Gaga has given her fans an outlet for their creativity and for their fan art. An exceptional feature is multilingual chat, which tears down linguistic barriers and gives everyone the chance to chat with other "little monsters" all over the world.

In substance, Littlemonsters is an online community of people united by a strong shared interest, a community that is open to other social networks, facilitates contact among fans, and promotes socially beneficial activism. And with its exclusive content, it generates and sustains a passion for pay-to-play that keeps bringing fans back to purchase music and tickets. Lady Gaga's manager, Troy Carter made an interesting comment: "There may come a day when you don't have the cover of *Vanity Fair*, or you may not be able to get on that big TV show. But it's important that you have that direct communication with that audience so they still know what you're doing." And if one day the one not to get the cover of *Vanity Fair* or the big TV show were Facebook?

CASE 4: LIVEPETITIONS

Livepetitions is the world's largest online petitioning site with a platform based in nine different countries. It is a social network that skilfully exploits the potential of social media as a means for access and a preferential channel for spreading messages.

Users access Livepetitions via Facebook using the OAuth protocol without having to fil out tedious forms. OAuth allows Livepetitions to receive certain information about its users: name and surname, photo, location, birthdate, email, and other data depending on the permissions enabled on Facebook.

When they sign a petition through their Facebook account, they become members of Firmiamo (Let's Sign), where the petitions are actually located. But an app is being developed that will allow users to read and sign the petition directly on Facebook.

Livepetitions exploits the viral mechanisms that are typical of social networks: for example, after a user has signed the petition, the new app asks the user if it can post an invitation to join the cause on a friend's timeline. The user is also prompted to spread word of the cause via email. Furthermore, in the version currently being developed, users can connect their Facebook and Twitter accounts to their Livepetitions account, as well as uploading a list of email addresses of people who should be contacted in the petition drive.

Livepetitions members are thus also its prime promoters. Sure, this is a strategy that works because of the nature of the particular site and its goals, but it can also be taken as a model and replicated, with the appropriate modifications and adaptations, to any proprietary company platform and specific communication strategy.

Image 45: Dashboard, the social platform for the Obama-Biden campaign

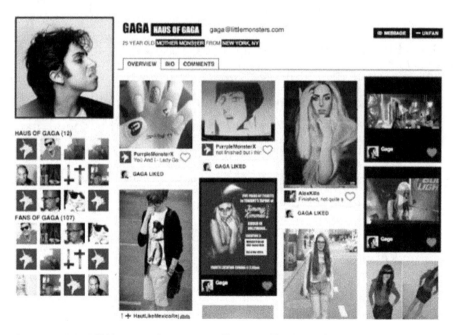

Image 46: Littlemonsters.com, the vertical social network dedicated to Lady Gaga fans

3.1.8. Is the Back Home Strategy for me?

Who should use the Back Home Strategy? Many, but not necessarily all. That should now be clear. It involves planning, designing and implementing a complex synergetic system and not all are in a position to afford it. However, I feel it is the only method that makes it possible to truly reap the full potential of social networks.

Large companies should begin to "think big" and not behave like small companies that unfortunately don't have the means to invest great amounts in concerted actions on a large scale. A food giant must not behave like a small restaurant. A large restaurant chain can implement the Back Home Strategy, and it will always give it a terrific advantage over its smaller cousins.

A small restaurant, on the other hand, can still set up its digital business with the free tools offered by social networks, such as fanpages. Naturally, it will have to cope with the problems we have discussed above: it will always risk losing contact with its customers or their data. However, a presence on social networks will help to make its name known.

SITOGRAPHY

www.socialmediatoday.com
www.cnn.com
www.wired.com
www.guardian.com
www.nastalenttalk.com
www.forbes.com
www.jeffbullas.com
www.commetrics.com
www.mashable.com
www.techcrunch.com
www.huffingtonpost.com
www.wikipedia.org
www.imediaconnection.com
www.google.com/adwords
www.insidefacebook.com
www.socialmediamonitoring.com
www.ticketmaster.com
www.connecting-managers.com
www.facebook.com/about/privacy
www.masternewmedia.org
www.allfacebook.com

Image 47: The beauty of Facebook

Alphabetical Index

www.ingramcontent.com/pod-product-compliance
Lightning Source LLC
LaVergne TN
LVHW022320060326
832902LV00020B/3569